Chavez

assigned ch. 1, 3, 5, 6

11 - classic ch. ants.
53 - tech. aids lots of institutions, including organizing events
72 - not clear that IWC is growing, but probably a sense in which they are a response to shift from dances to markets —

— claim that there is fastest-growing segment of Amer. Xtianty is not supported anywhere —

— value of the book is its analysis of these groups/orgs. Claim that it is fast-growing is not supported, so all attempts to connect the descriptive elements to explanation of growth/attractiveness are misguided —

162 — huge problem of not comparing people/resources across whole. types of relig. cf. largest of IWC groups to typical cong is not way to assess overall appeal/presence in the society —

— there is a big contrast between IWC + church planters who prioritize finding a place to meet — cf. Martí description of Schuller's beginnings in Orange Grove, looking for a place to meet

D1559435

THE RISE OF NETWORK CHRISTIANITY

GLOBAL PENTECOSTAL AND CHARISMATIC
CHRISTIANITY
Series Editor
Donald E. Miller
Executive Director, Center for Religion and Civic Culture,
University of Southern California

THE RISE OF NETWORK CHRISTIANITY

HOW INDEPENDENT LEADERS ARE CHANGING THE RELIGIOUS LANDSCAPE

BRAD CHRISTERSON
AND
RICHARD FLORY

OXFORD
UNIVERSITY PRESS

Oxford University Press is a department of the University of Oxford. It furthers
the University's objective of excellence in research, scholarship, and education
by publishing worldwide. Oxford is a registered trade mark of Oxford University
Press in the UK and certain other countries.

Published in the United States of America by Oxford University Press
198 Madison Avenue, New York, NY 10016, United States of America.

Library of Congress Cataloging-in-Publication Data
Names: Christerson, Brad, author. | Flory, Richard, author.
Title: The rise of network christianity : how independent leaders
are changing the religious landscape / Brad Christerson and Richard Flory.
Description: New York, NY : Oxford University Press, [2017]
Identifiers: LCCN 2016032130 (print) | LCCN 2016048398 (ebook) |
ISBN 9780190635671 (hardback) | ISBN 9780190635688 (updf) |
ISBN 9780190635695 (epub) | ISBN 9780190635701 (online content)
Subjects: LCSH: Pentecostalism—History—21st century.
Classification: LCC BR1644 .C446 2017 (print) | LCC BR1644 (ebook) |
DDC 277.3/083—dc23
LC record available at https://lccn.loc.gov/2016032130

CONTENTS

ACKNOWLEDGMENTS

This book has its origins in the Pentecostal and Charismatic Research Initiative (PCRI), which was housed at the Center for Religion and Civic Culture (CRCC) at the University of Southern California and funded by the John Templeton Foundation. The goal of PCRI was to investigate different expressions of Pentecostalism, focusing primarily on understanding its growth and vitality in the global south and east. But PCRI also included a project in which several scholars at CRCC focused on Pentecostal and Charismatic religion in Los Angeles, the city that has been called the "cradle" of the global Pentecostal movement. In this, we were particularly interested in understanding what Pentecostalism looks like in Los Angeles, some 100 or so years after it emerged at the Azusa Street Mission, and whether LA is still an important center of Pentecostal activity. Our Los Angeles research eventually led us to new centers of Pentecostal activity such as Redding California and Kansas City. This book is one result of that effort.

Throughout our research and writing efforts, we have had many conversations about Pentecostalism, why it is important, and how best to understand it. Many of these conversations took place in typical academic settings such as our research group at CRCC or in professional meetings. But we also engaged in these conversations in very atypical places such as when we were out surfing or meeting at O'Malley's Irish Pub, our "office away from the office." Perhaps most memorably we had what was essentially one long conversation about the groups we were studying over the course of a thousand-mile road trip from L.A. to Redding California, and back.

We have benefited tremendously from different colleagues who have supported our efforts, provided critical input, and, in general, kept us committed to completing the task. Many different people have read all or part of this book or have heard presentations from different portions of it. We are particularly indebted to three anonymous reviewers for their comments at the proposal stage and when the manuscript was complete. Their comments, whether followed or not, have improved the final product.

We are grateful to the leaders and participants of the groups and ministries documented in this book, who graciously gave us their time and were very candid in explaining their faith, their activities, and the nuts and bolts of the ministries they lead and participate in. Without their willingness to openly share their time, ideas, and experiences with us, this book would not have been possible.

We are also grateful to those who assisted in our research efforts, including colleagues, friends, and current and former students who shared their own personal experiences, insights, and opened doors to interviews with high-profile leaders and their followers. Special thanks to Doretha O'Quinn, Pete Menjares, Clint Arnold, Chelsea Tonti, Lauren Frey, Maggie Hazen, and Tabitha Coe for your generousity in sharing your time and connections.

Most important, we are indebted to the creative and collaborative environment of CRCC, without which this book would not exist. In particular, we thank Donald E. Miller, who originated and developed PCRI, Brie Loskota, and the rest of the CRCC staff for always supporting—and prodding—us as we worked to complete this book. And special thanks to Nick Street, senior writer at CRCC, who deftly edited our prose, making this a better book than it would have been otherwise. We are also grateful to the John Templeton Foundation for generously supporting the research efforts represented in this book and the entire PCRI project.

Last, and certainly not least, we are especially grateful for all the love and support of Carin and Malia in this and all of our endeavors.

CHAPTER ONE

THE RISE OF "INDEPENDENT NETWORK CHARISMATIC" CHRISTIANITY

In January 2011, more than 30,000 people packed Reliant Stadium in Houston, Texas. But they weren't there for football. Instead, they had come for an event called "The Response: A Call to Prayer for a Nation in Crisis."

The crowd cheered wildly as then—US presidential candidate and Texas Governor Rick Perry walked to the center of the stage. Perry quoted the Bible and preached about the spiritual salvation that comes from Jesus Christ, then concluded with a prayer for a country he believed to be overwhelmed by problems: "We see discord at home. We see fear in the marketplace. We see anger in the halls of government." Perry asked God to forgive the American people for forgetting "who made us, who protects us, and who blesses us." In response, the crowd exploded into cheers and praises to God.

More than five years later and 1,500 miles away, at the Los Angeles Memorial Coliseum, more than 50,000 people gathered to, in the words of the prophet and "intercessor" Lou Engle, usher in a "third great awakening" in America through the outpouring of the Holy Spirit. The event, Azusa Now, was named for the 1906 Azusa Street Revival, which is often considered the birth of Pentecostalism. Azusa Now lasted more than sixteen hours and featured some of the most popular Charismatic (emphasizing miracles and manifestations of the Holy Spirit) Christian leaders in world. There was lively worship music and preaching. But most notable were the hundreds of people who claimed they were healed from various diseases and disabilities and many more who said they received direct "words of knowledge" from God.

Although not in any way directly connected, these two events and the leaders who organized them are key components of a movement that some Charismatic leaders (see, for example, Wagner 2010) are calling a "new Reformation." The fastest-growing movement in Christianity, both in the West and in the global South, is now led by a network of dynamic independent religious entrepreneurs, often referred to as "apostles."

These leaders have gained attention in the United States recently, primarily through their relationships with conservative politicians like Ted Cruz, Sarah Palin, Newt Gingrich, Bobby Jindal, and Rick Perry. With the exception of Palin, these politicians do not attend or partici- pate in Charismatic churches or ministries, but they have connections to Charismatic apostles who see them as vehicles through which they can remake America. This network of Charismatic leaders is not only trying to save individual souls, but to create a "heaven on earth" where poverty, war, violence, and disease no longer exist.

This book explores this fast-growing, closely connected move- ment of religious entrepreneurs that we call "Independent Network Charismatic" (INC) Christianity. We examine these leaders and their ministries and attempt to explain why they are rapidly gaining fol- lowers in the United States. The rise of INC Christianity, we argue, is symptomatic of larger, macro-structural changes in American society, and as a result other American religious traditions will likely take on some of the characteristics of INC Christianity in the near future.

The Changing American Religious Landscape

Religious belief and practice are undergoing profound change in the United States, particularly among young adults. Recent research has shown that young adults between the ages of eighteen and thirty have the lowest levels of religious affiliation and participation of any age

Table 1.1 Affiliates and Growth Rates for Broad Christian Traditions–US 1970–2010

Christian Tradition	Number of Affiliates 2010 (Thousands)	Avg. Annual Growth 1970–2010 (%)
Roman Catholic	70,656	0.96
Orthodox	6,253	0.89
Protestant	56,015	−0.05
Anglican	2,191	−0.94
Independent	68,492	1.37%

Source: World Christian Database.

weird source for this

group in the country, and they are significantly less likely to be affiliated with a religion than their parents' and grandparents' generations were at the same age (Pew Research Center 2012). Nearly one in five adults under the age of thirty says he or she was raised in a religion but is now unaffiliated with any particular faith (Pew Research Center 2012). In the current General Social Survey (GSS) nearly one quarter of Americans between the ages of eighteen and twenty-nine have described their religion as "none," compared with just 12 percent in the 1970s and 1980s. Young adults are also less likely to attend religious services than older generations. Eighteen percent of young adults today attend church weekly or nearly weekly compared with 26 percent of young adults who did so in the late 1970s (Pew Research Center 2012).

Tables 1.1 and 1.2 also show a major shift in the patterns of American religious affiliation. These data were drawn from the World Christian Database (WCD), which tracks the number of "affiliates," or people who are either members or regular attenders of different types of congregations, from 1970 to 2010. We see three historic shifts:

1) *The decline of Protestantism.* Throughout the history of the United States, Protestant Christianity has been the dominant religious tradition. This is no longer the case. In 1970, the broad tradition of Protestantism had the largest number of affiliates

Table 1.2 Affiliates and Growth Rates for Various Christian Subgroups–US 1970–2010

Subgroup	Number of Affiliates 2010 (Thousands)	Avg. Annual Growth 1970–2010 (%)
Evangelical (Protestant)	51,297	.63
Pentecostal (Protestant)	6,191	2.95
Neo-Charismatic (Independent)	36,302	3.24
Apostolic/Pentecostal Apostolic (Independent)	341	3.66
Presbyterian	4,180	−0.9
Methodist	7,799	−1.51
Lutheran	7,394	−0.53

Source: World Christian Database.

(members or regular attenders of a Protestant congregation) at just over 57 million, followed by Roman Catholicism at just over 48 million. Forty years later, the number of people affiliated with Protestant congregations had shrunk to approximately 56 million. When one considers that the American population as a whole grew an average of 1 percent a year during those four decades, adding over 100 million people by 2010, the Protestant decline is even more striking. Anglicans, which include Episcopalians (and were not included as Protestants in the WCD data), shrunk even faster, at almost 1 percent per year.

Table 1.2 shows the growth/decline rates for selected subgroups of Protestants. This table shows that much of the decline during this time came from mainline Protestantism, most notably the largest mainline denominations: Methodist, Presbyterian, and Lutheran. Evangelicals grew in numbers during this time by an average of .63 percent per year. This evangelical growth rate, however, is smaller than the 1 percent per year growth rate of the population, meaning that evangelicals shrunk as a percentage of the American population between 1970 and 2010, from

19 percent to 16 percent. Pentecostals were the only denominational group defined as Protestant in the WCD that grew faster than the growth of the overall population during that time.

2) *The decline of denominational Christianity and the rise of independents.* Another historic shift during this period is the relative decline of affiliates to denominational congregations, including Roman Catholic, Orthodox, Protestant, and Anglican Christianity, and the concurrent growth of those affiliated with nondenominational independent congregations. Table 1.1 shows that denominational Protestants and Anglicans declined the most, with their absolute numbers shrinking by an average of .05 percent and .94 percent per year, respectively.

The number of those affiliated with Roman Catholic and Orthodox congregations grew in absolute numbers, but they also shrunk as a percentage of the total population because their average annual growth rates were less than the overall population growth rate. Meanwhile, the only major categories of Protestants that grew faster than the overall population were those not associated with a denomination—independents. Affiliates of neo-Charismatic congregations accounted for the largest percentage of this growth.

3) *The growth of Pentecostal/Charismatic believers.* Table 1.2 shows that the fastest-growing group of Christians in America from 1970 to 2010 attended either Pentecostal or Charismatic congregations. The fastest-growing subcategories of Pentecostal/ Charismatic Christians were neo-Charismatics (defined as those affiliated with a Charismatic congregation that is not connected with a denomination) and Apostolic (defined as affiliates of congregations that emphasize "living apostles, prophets and other Charismatic officials)." Their growth rates are phenomenal, considering that most other Christian groups shrunk as a percentage of the overall population during this forty-year period. Although Catholics, denominational Protestants, and Evangelicals are still larger than these groups, if current growth rates continue, Pentecostals and Charismatics will soon outnumber all of them.

This book aims to explain the phenomenal growth rates of one particular subgroup of independent neo-Charismatic believers that we have labeled "Independent Network Charismatic." We believe that this group is the fastest-growing Christian subgroup in America and that its unique practices and governance structures account for its success in the American religious marketplace.

RESEARCH METHODS

We began our research with a broad question: "Are there new fast-growing movements in Pentecostal and Charismatic Christianity in the United States, and, if so, why are they growing?"

To find out, we first conducted in-depth interviews with ten current and former leaders within established Pentecostal and Charismatic denominations and organizations. In our interviews, a consensus emerged that the fastest-growing new groups were independent Charismatic ministries led by high-profile leaders. These leaders had their roots in Pentecostalism but had broken their ties with established groups and denominations. We eventually labeled them "Independent Network Charismatic" or INC.

We decided to focus our research primarily on four of the most frequently mentioned groups—Bethel, International House of Prayer (IHOP), Harvest International Ministries (HIM), and the Wagner Leadership Institute. To supplement, we also conducted interviews with leaders and participants at other large and/or fast-growing INC ministries, including, among others, Youth With a Mission (YWAM). In total, we conducted a total of forty-one in-depth interviews with senior leaders, staff, and current and former participants in INC Christian ministries. We also attended multiple events, conferences, leadership training events, and on-site visits from 2009 to 2016.

After transcribing these interviews, we analyzed our data to look for patterns in six areas: 1) how ministries were established, 2) governance, 3) beliefs and practices, 4) finances and promotion, 5) reasons given for growth, and 6) difficulties and potential threats to growth.

The patterns we found in these six areas became the foundation for this book.

DEFINING THE TERMS

Pentecostal/Charismatic Christianity has numerous branches, many of which overlap in their theology and practice. The groups and leaders that we call INC Christianity, however, have broken off from the rest of Pentecostal/Charismatic Christianity in significant ways. Thus, as a starting point, we need to define the terms that describe the various strands of Pentecostal/Charismatic Christianity.

If one were to combine all Pentecostal/Charismatic believers, the resulting group would arguably be the largest Protestant Christian movement in the world, with an estimated half-a-billion followers worldwide (Miller et al. 2007 Poloma 2003). An emphasis on the "gifts of the Holy Spirit," including glossolalia (speaking in tongues), healing, prophecy, and other supernatural miracles, distinguishes Pentecostal/Charismatic Christianity from other traditions. There are further distinctions among the various Pentecostal/Charismatic branches that are important to the arguments that we make in this book.

In North America, the term Pentecostal typically refers to the denominational groups that emerged from Los Angeles's Azusa Street Revival in 1906 and that grew rapidly in the first three decades of the twentieth century (Poloma 2003). The Assemblies of God (predominantly white) and the Church of God in Christ (predominantly African American) denominations developed from what was originally a multiracial revival movement. These two denominations, along with the Church of God (Cleveland, Tennessee) and the International Church of the Foursquare Gospel are the largest Pentecostal denominations in North America. These denominational groups are also called "first wave" Pentecostals, and most emerged in the first quarter of the twentieth century (Poloma 2003).

The term Charismatic emerged to describe believers who remained within mainline (including Catholic) and independent churches but embraced the Pentecostal emphasis on the gifts of the Spirit but who were not part of Pentecostal denominations. This movement grew rapidly in the postwar period and eventually encompassed significant minorities of evangelical Protestants (23 percent), mainline Protestants (9 percent), Roman Catholics (13 percent), and black Protestants (36 percent) (Poloma 2003; Green et al. 1997). Some scholars refer to these Charismatics as "second wave" Pentecostals because they emerged after World War II, long after the first wave denominations were established (Poloma 2003).

The term "neo-Charismatic" (also known as "third wave" Charismatic) refers to believers who are involved in independent Charismatic churches and ministries that were established after 1970. Miller (1997) refers to these as "new paradigm" churches, and includes movements such as Vineyard, Calvary Chapel, and Hope Chapel in this category. The groups and leaders that we describe in this book would fall under the category of neo-Charismatic but differ in important ways from the new paradigm churches:

1) *They do not seek to build a "movement"* or to create affiliated franchise congregations using a particular name.
2) *They are not primarily focused on building congregations* in the traditional sense, but rather seek to influence the beliefs and practices of believers regardless of congregation or affiliation, including those who are not affiliated with any congregation or religious group.
3) *They seek to transform society as a whole* rather than saving individual souls and building the church.
4) Instead of being formally organized into a "movement" or "denomination" *the various leaders and ministries in this category are highly connected by networks of cooperation.*

C. Peter Wagner, an influential writer and scholar in the Charismatic world and a highly influential INC leader himself, has coined the term the "New Apostolic Reformation" (NAR) to describe many of the leaders and ministries that we are calling Independent Network Charismatic. The fast-growing WCD categories—Apostolic/Pentecostal Apostolic and neo-Charismatic (see Table 1.2)—include many of Wagner's NAR groups. Wagner sees these leaders and their ministries as representing a historic shift in the way Christianity is organized and practiced, so much so that he compares this shift to the Protestant Reformation. In his 2006 book *Apostles Today* Wagner writes:

> It is a "reformation" because we are currently witnessing the most radical change in the way of "doing church" since the Protestant Reformation. It is "apostolic" because the recognition of the gift and office of apostle is the most radical of a whole list of changes from the old wineskin. And it is "new" to distinguish it from several older traditional church groups that have incorporated the term "apostolic" into their official name ... Protestant denominationalism over the past 500 years has been, for the most part governed by teachers and administrators rather than by apostles and prophets.

Wagner goes on to describe the difference between this traditional denominational administrator/congregational teacher model and the "apostolic" model of leadership:

> In traditional denominations the locus of authority is ordinarily found in groups, not in individuals. That is why we are accustomed to hearing about deacon boards, boards of trustees, presbyteries, general assemblies, and so on. In the New Apostolic Reformation, however, trust has shifted from groups to individuals. On the local church level, the pastor now functions as the leader of the church instead of as an employee of the church. On the translocal level, the apostle is the one who has earned the trust of the pastors and other leaders; and trust inevitably imparts authority (Wagner 2006).

According to Wagner, the primary difference between a traditional denominational–congregational model and the NAR model of leadership is that apostles—highly influential dynamic individuals who "exude authority" and are able to bring about miracles of the Spirit—are now taking control of the governance from denominations and other administrative bureaucracies. He sees this development as wholly positive and more consistent with the biblical leadership roles of "apostle and prophet."

Wagner and some of his critics (see Geivett and Pivec 2014; MacArthur 2013) have made connections between NAR and the controversial "Latter Rain" movement in the late 1940s. This movement, led by George Hawtin and Herric Holt in North Battleford, Saskatchewan, emphasized relational networks over bureaucratic structures, the restoration of the offices of apostle and prophet, and a renewed emphasis on healing, prophecy, and supernatural manifestations of the Holy Spirit (Wilkinson and Althouse 2014). These are the hallmarks of the INC groups that we describe in this book. As might be expected, because the Latter Rain movement shunned formal organizations and denominations, the movement did not lead to any lasting formal institutions, but its influence on current neo-Charismatic belief and practice is evident in INC Christianity.

We have decided not to use Wagner's label NAR for the groups that we describe in this book, although Wagner and other NAR enthusiasts would argue that all of the groups that we describe would fall under his definition. We use our INC label instead because 1) some of the leaders and groups we studied do not want to be associated with the NAR and 2) some of the groups we studied differ enough in their beliefs and practices from the dominant NAR groups as to be distinct from the NAR. In short, all NAR groups would fall within the category of INC, but not all INC groups are part of NAR. *based on what?*

Geivett and Pivec (2014) estimate that 3 million people regularly attend NAR-influenced congregations in the United States, and that number is growing faster than that of any other segment of American Christianity. They also claim that the largest churches in the world are neo-Charismatic and influenced by NAR teachings, including David Yonggi Cho's Yoido Full Gospel Church in South Korea (1 million members), E.A. Adeboye's Redeemed Christian Church of God in Nigeria (5 million members), Cesar Castellano's International Charismatic Mission in Bogota, Colombia (250,000), and Embassy of the Blessed Kingdom of God for All Nations in Ukraine (20,000).

Newsweek magazine recently named Adeboye one of the fifty most powerful people in the world (Geivett and Pivec 2014).

We think that INC Christianity is important, not only because of its numbers and growth rate, but because it represents a new form of Christianity that could reshape the global religious landscape for years to come. It has unique features that, although not entirely new, have not been seen on such a large scale before. Organizationally, it is composed of networks of dynamic individual leaders rather than of congregations and denominations. These leaders are adamant that their goal is not to build a "movement" or "organization" but rather to exert their influence through media, conferences, and their relationships with other individual leaders in religious and secular professions. Thus it is not a "church," "movement," "sect," or "denomination." These words suggest a level of formal organization that simply does not exist in INC Christianity. Rather, INC Christianity is at its core simply a collection of strong leaders who know each other and combine and recombine for specific projects, but who are functionally independent of one another.

Their individual revenue streams flow directly to them and their ministries, and they have full discretion over how to use them. They receive direct "words from the Lord" that dictate their decisions rather than relying on a consensus-based process with other believers. These leaders gain their legitimacy and influence from their perceived ability to access supernatural power to produce "signs and wonders" rather than through speaking ability, educational credentials, or position in a hierarchy.

Likewise, INC followers are not necessarily members of congregations in the traditional sense. They often move from conference to conference, ministry school to ministry school, and define their faith more by their practices and allegiance to an individual leader than by their connection with a congregation, denomination, or tradition.

INC leaders are also distinctive in their beliefs and practices. They emphasize practice over belief, and those practices they deem most important are largely absent from traditional Protestantism. Specifically, prophecy (receiving direct words from God), physical healing, and deliverance from evil spirits are the practices that define most INC practitioners. Many (though not all) INC leaders are also postmillennial in their theological orientation, meaning that they believe that the power of God is available now to usher in the "new kingdom of God," creating a heaven on earth in the here and now. This postmillennial utopianism is a break from classical Pentecostal theology, which is focused on building up the church and saving souls for the next life.

THEORETICAL STARTING POINTS

Our study seeks to explain the rapid growth of INC Christianity and explore its implications for the future of religion. Our analysis is framed primarily by the "religious economies" paradigm in sociology, which holds that in democracies where there is no official state religion, there is a "marketplace" in which religious "firms" compete with each other for "customers." Roger Finke and Rodney Stark (1992) describe the paradigm this way:

> Religious economies are like commercial economies in that they consist of a market made up of a set of current and potential customers and a set of firms seeking to serve that market. The fate of these firms will depend on 1) aspects of their organizational structure, 2) their sales representatives, 3) their product, and 4) their marketing techniques. Translated into more churchly language, the relative success of religious bodies (especially when confronted with an unregulated economy) will depend upon their polity, their clergy, their religious doctrines, and their evangelization techniques.

As Finke and Stark (1992) note, religious disestablishment creates opportunities for religious "entrepreneurs" to compete for customers who, at least legally, are allowed to join whatever faith they chose. The religious "goods" that religious "firms" provide are typically promises of future rewards, supernatural explanations for life events, meaning, and a sense of belonging (Sherkat and Ellison 1999; Stark and Bainbridge 1987).

Our analysis suggests that INC leaders have expanded their "market share" because of their innovative organizational structures, unique "product" offerings, and inventive methods of marketing and financing their activities, all of which leverage the power of digital communications technologies.

Some critics point out that using an economic framework to explain the success of religious groups can become an exercise in untestable circular reasoning that goes something like this: "Why are these religious groups successful? Because they offer what people want, given the context. What do people want, given the context? What these groups offer."

We agree that this sometimes is true, but we avoid this formulation by identifying unique aspects of INC Christianity that explain their market success and hypothesize that religious groups of any stripe that include these features will grow faster than those that do not.

INC leaders and their ministries have their origins in the neo-Charismatic movements of the 1970s. In his 1997 book *Reinventing American Protestantism,* Donald Miller concludes that the new paradigm movements represent a possible "second reformation" or third "great awakening." He demonstrates that these movements reject the overly bureaucratic rules and procedures of mainline denominations, seek to restore the "priesthood of all believers," emphasize "unmediated communication between an individual and God," and "direct access to the realm of the supernatural which more domesticated forms of religion, over time, have found increasingly unseemly and magical" (Miller 1997).

Miller argues, following Max Weber, that the mainline Protestant denominations have become progressively routinized over time, which has led to their decline:

> Priestly roles are identified, sacred texts are canonized, rules and procedures for mediating access to the sacred evolve, and in this process the people become more and more distanced from the transforming source of the sacred. Taken to an extreme, religious institutions become encrusted bureaucracies that survive with low levels of commitment,

primarily through habit and because they are integrated with other aspects of institutional life (Miller 1997).

The neo-Charismatic groups in Miller's study avoided this routinization by offering unmediated access to the supernatural and by cultivating dynamic leaders who work outside the institutional rules and practices of established denominations. However, what we have found in our research is that, since Miller's book was written, those new paradigm movements have themselves begun to routinize, establishing rules and procedures for mediating access to the supernatural, as well as founding a formal denomination (in the case of the Vineyard) and implementing regulatory structures that control the beliefs and practices of the congregations that bear their name. These groups have also grown much more slowly since Miller's book was written.

Since the mid-1990s, the new set of less routinized groups that we are calling INC Christianity have emerged to take the place of the new paradigm churches as the fastest-growing edge of Protestantism. These new groups retain many of the features of the founding neo-Charismatic groups, but have reconfigured their organizational forms, beliefs, practices, and marketing techniques—all of which, we will argue, have led to much greater growth potential, particularly among young people.

THE POST-1970 SOCIAL CONTEXT

In the following chapters, we make the case that INC Christianity is uniquely well suited to grow in the current American social context. Many social theorists assert that in the last four decades or so, fundamental changes have altered the macrostructure of society. We think that these social changes have led to the transformation of the religious marketplace in the United States and other developed Western nations. We also think that these changes give INC Christianity significant advantages that can at least partially explain its growing market share in the current religious economy.

Three macrolevel social changes have occurred since 1970 that we think are especially important in explaining the rise of INC Christianity:

1) *Globalization.* It has become accepted in academia that advances in transportation and communications technologies have accelerated the integration of social processes and systems (economic, political, cultural) across national boundaries.

2) *The digital revolution.* Advances in digital technology, most notably the microcomputer and the Internet, have transformed the dissemination and communication of information, which has expanded and democratized access to knowledge and information.

3) *The rise of networks and the decline of bureaucracies.* Related to the previously mentioned changes, organizational theorists have documented a shift from large-scale hierarchical organizations toward informal social systems organized by networks of small-scale actors. In a number of industries, the coordination of complex production processes is moving away from large vertically integrated hierarchical firms toward a more flexible form of governance consisting of networks of small firms and individuals that can combine and recombine for short-term tasks in response to changing market conditions. Advances in information technology make this form of organization possible on a global scale.

These large-scale social changes have produced changes in the religious marketplace, particularly for younger adults. These changes can be summarized as follows:

1) *An increase in cultural and religious pluralism.* Globalization has exposed us all to multiple cultures and worldviews. Immigration has made even the most monochromatic postwar American suburbs increasingly multicultural. As a result, young children grow up around neighbors with multiple religious and cultural perspectives. Access to an increasingly globalized social media

environment also allows for the exploration of different ideas and perspectives at the tap of a screen. Increasingly, religious affiliation is less "taken for granted" as people are able to explore and choose their own religious orientation through a rapidly expanding array of religious choices. As a result, religious groups must compete harder to recruit and retain each subsequent generation, making the religious economy much more unstable and competitive.

2) *Interactive media.* Access to information is now both instant and interactive rather than time consuming and passive. People are now active creators of media images and information as well as consumers. This affects the religious marketplace in two ways. First, believers increasingly expect to be active participants in religious activities rather than passive consumers of religious information. They not only want to choose from a variety of religious options; they also want to actively participate in and shape the religious "product." Second, they are less likely to be impressed by or be a satisfied "consumer" of the sermons or activities of their local congregation when the sermons, blogs, or live-streamed activities of more interesting speakers or more spectacular events around the world are easily available.

really? not what megas are about

3) *Declining loyalty to institutions.* As previously noted, globalization and the information revolution have caused large-scale institutions to decline relative to flexible networks of individual leaders and smaller organizations. In the realm of religion, instant access to multiple worldviews and religious products means that believers can "pick and choose" from an array of products and activities that come from multiple sources. No longer does one need to commit to a particular tradition or congregation in order to access religious "goods." One may attend a denominational congregation for a particular reason, but may also be influenced more by a live-streamed celebrity preacher or attendance at a high-intensity religious conference. In addition, instant access to information and alternative sources of advice and activities means that a believer's loyalty

is typically divided among multiple religious "outlets." Also, instant media access and the 24/7 news cycle have made the flaws and scandals of large-scale institutions more visible. Thus a religious scandal that takes place in a large religious institution—like the Catholic Church, for example—may create more cynicism toward large religious bureaucracies.

In the following chapters, we make the case that these changes have increased the potential market share for religious activity organized by networks of innovative religious entrepreneurs, as opposed to the traditional offerings of formal religious organizations. We think we are seeing the beginning of a shift in the way that religious "goods" are produced and distributed, which will change the way people experience and practice religion in the future.

More specifically, we expect to see the unique elements of INC Christianity spread to other religious traditions and grow more dominant. There will always be a market niche for traditionally organized congregations and denominations. Our argument, however, is that this niche will grow smaller, while the market share of religious goods produced by networks of religious entrepreneurs will expand steadily because they are more closely suited to the current social context in which they operate.

In the following chapters, we examine the origins, governance structures, religious products, and the marketing and financing strategies of INC Christianity. We also examine the competitive advantages as well as the disadvantages of INC Christianity in the current religious economy. We conclude by proposing a theoretical explanation for the rise of INC Christianity and speculate as to what this dramatic development may mean for the future of Protestant Christianity in particular and religious belief and practice in general.

CHAPTER TWO

THE ORIGINS OF INC CHRISTIANITY

Where did these fast-growing ministries come from? Who are their innovative leaders? What makes them so attractive? To answer these questions we need to examine the origins of the leaders and ministries that constitute INC Christianity. It is important to understand the connections between the founders of INC Christianity and "third wave" neo-Charismatic Christianity. The two share many similarities, and, interestingly, most INC leaders have some connection to one third wave pioneer in particular—John Wimber, who seemed uniquely gifted at influencing others and producing "signs and wonders" (miraculous events and supernatural phenomena). Exploring the events, conflicts, and organizational schisms that eventually led INC leaders to part ways with the movements that had shaped them is key to understanding the social and organizational impetus behind their emergence and their success.

The INC leaders we describe in this book can trace their roots to the "new paradigm" movements (primarily Calvary Chapel and Vineyard) described by Miller (1997). In this brief overview, we highlight key events and decisions that were critical in the break between INC leaders and their third wave predecessors.

CHUCK SMITH, JOHN WIMBER, AND THE THIRD WAVE

Chuck Smith founded Calvary Chapel in 1965. Smith, a former Foursquare pastor in Southern California, felt that the rules and procedures of the Foursquare denomination prevented him from taking his ministry in the directions he wanted to go. In fact, he began to question the value of denominations as a whole and saw them as places where power-oriented bureaucrats marginalized dynamic leaders by "surrounding themselves with weaker men and by eliminating those who are a threat to their position" (quoted in Miller 1997).

After starting a successful independent church in Corona, Smith felt God calling him to a struggling congregation of twenty-five people in Costa Mesa. He welcomed young people into the church and subsequently met a man named Lonnie Frisbee, a recent Charismatic convert who was coming out of the drug culture of the 1960s. Frisbee had not only an intense zeal for evangelism, but also reportedly had tremendous capacity to access supernatural divine powers to heal people. Smith's connection with Frisbee, who became central to the "Jesus People Movement" (DiSabatino 1999), brought masses of young people from the surf and drug culture in Southern California to Smith's Calvary Chapel Costa Mesa, which quickly exploded into a large, thriving church of several thousand young people seeking spiritual guidance.

A group of Smith's young disciples (known as "sons" of Chuck Smith)—including Raul Reis, Jeff Johnson, Mike McIntosh, and Greg Laurie—began planting highly successful Calvary Chapel megachurches all over Southern California, replicating Smith's combination of popular-music-inspired worship, informal style, literalist Bible preaching, and openness to the miraculous manifestations of the Holy Spirit. In the 1970s, a former Quaker named John Wimber joined the Calvary Chapel movement and became highly influential among the INC leaders whom we document in this book.

Wimber, a professional musician (whom some have credited with bringing together the Righteous Brothers), became a Christian in his late twenties and joined Yorba Linda Friends Church (Friends is another term for Quakers) in Orange County in 1962, where he became an adult Sunday School teacher and Bible study leader—and eventually the pastor, for a short time. Similar to Smith, he became frustrated with the administrative and bureaucratic aspects of pastoring a denominational church. In 1974 he was hired by C. Peter Wagner, of Fuller Theological Seminary, to create the Charles E. Fuller Institute of Evangelism and Church Growth within the Fuller Evangelistic Association, which was headed by Wagner at the time (Kraft 2005).

While at Fuller, Wimber began to learn about and experiment with the gifts of the Holy Spirit. A number of the professors in the School of World Mission had served as missionaries in non-Western countries and had experienced various manifestations of the supernatural in those contexts. Wimber learned of their experiences and also studied many Charismatic leaders and churches as part of his research on church growth (Miller 1997). During this time he came in contact with Calvary Chapel "afterglows," which were meetings in private homes to explore manifestations of the Holy Spirit such as healing and speaking in tongues (Calvary Chapel churches generally avoid tongues and other manifestations of the Spirit in their Sunday church services).

Having experienced the Holy Spirit in tangible ways in these meetings, Wimber in 1977 wanted to start a congregation that was more experimental in its engagement with the Holy Spirit than his Friends church. He began leading services in a building across from the Yorba Linda Friends Church, and the group quickly grew into a 1,500-member congregation that Wimber affiliated with Calvary Chapel and named Calvary Chapel Yorba Linda (Miller 1997).

In 1982, Wimber attended a meeting with Chuck Smith and a number of other highly successful Calvary Chapel pastors, including Raul Reis, Jeff Johnson, Greg Laurie, and Mike McIntosh. This meeting would change the trajectory of Wimber, Calvary Chapel, and the budding neo-Charismatic movement as a whole. This group became concerned that Wimber's experimental approach to the Holy Spirit left too much room for error and chaos. A former Calvary Chapel leader described this fateful gathering this way:

> It happened in a particular series of meetings up in the mountains over a two-day period. One of the pastors there made the statement, "Look, when you go to a McDonald's, you know you can order a Big Mac. If

someone walks into a Calvary Chapel, they should be able to know what's there. They shouldn't get any doctrinal surprises." In other words, he was arguing for the standardization of the Calvary Chapels.

According to the former Calvary Chapel leader just quoted, it was this meeting that led to John Wimber's split with Chuck Smith and the Calvary Chapel fellowship and to his decision to join Ken Gullickson's Vineyard movement. According to several former leaders we interviewed, following this meeting, Calvary Chapel become much less open to theological disagreements and less comfortable with experimental approaches to engaging the Holy Spirit. One former Calvary Chapel leader said,

> I think what [the Calvary Chapel break with Wimber] did was kind of institutionalize a conservatism towards the Holy Spirit, not a rejection of him, not a stopping of the gifts, nothing like that. [Calvary Chapel] didn't suddenly become cessationist. But I think it institutionalized the cautiousness.

According to these leaders, after the break with Wimber, Calvary Chapel became more focused on regulating their affiliated churches in terms of theology and practice, and more oriented toward establishing what they were against theologically and politically rather than toward what they wanted to become. Wimber, on the other hand, free from the scrutiny that being affiliated with Calvary entailed, continued his much more experimental approach to the Holy Spirit.

Wimber's Vineyard (formerly Calvary Chapel) church in Yorba Linda continued to grow, and in 1983 it moved to a large 65,000-square-foot warehouse in Anaheim and changed its name to Anaheim Vineyard. Wimber also began to team-teach a class with C. Peter Wagner and Charles Kraft at Fuller Seminary called "Signs, Wonders and Church Growth," which would become legendary in the neo-Charismatic movement. More than 800 students took the course during the time it was offered at Fuller, from 1982 to 1985, breaking all Fuller enrollment records (Kraft 2005).

In the course, Wimber would lead students in the practices of prophecy and healing. Typically, he would ask the class to be quiet and listen for God to speak to them. Often a student would report that God revealed something specific about somebody whom He wanted to heal. Wimber would ask if anyone in the class fit that description. They would then ask that God heal the person. According to reports, many students themselves were healed from physical ailments during this class.

It was through this class that Wimber's fellow Fuller professors C. Peter Wagner and Charles Kraft became convinced of the miraculous power available through the Holy Spirit (Kraft 2005; Wagner 2010). Wimber also held conferences on miraculous signs and wonders all over the world, and his notoriety and influence grew during the 1980s. During this time, Wimber's Anaheim Vineyard continued to grow rapidly.

In the late 1980s and early 1990s, Wimber and the Vineyard became embroiled in controversy because of their relationship with two different entities—the "Kansas City Prophets" and the leaders of the "Toronto Blessing." These associations led to yet another set of developments that are crucial to understanding the INC leaders and ministries that we describe in this book.

The Kansas City Prophets included Bob Jones (not the same Bob Jones affiliated with Bob Jones University), John Paul Jackson, Paul Cain, and Mike Bickle—all of whom were based in Kansas City. These modern-day "prophets" declared that the End Times were coming and that believers needed to listen to them to get instructions directly from God to be ready for the return of Jesus. Wimber began traveling and speaking with these prophets at conferences, causing concern among some Vineyard leaders and among Pentecostal denominational leaders. According to a former Vineyard leader, a high-profile figure in a Pentecostal denomination pleaded with Wimber to disassociate from the Kansas City Prophets:

He said, "John, whatever you do, I know what this is. Don't put these guys on your platform. You're going to regret this." I remember, I think it was a phone meeting, we got off the phone with [the well-known leader], and John looked at me and said, "You know, I have a feeling he's right, but God told me to do it, and we're going to do it anyway." And that was a major, major turning point in the history of the Vineyard and in my humble opinion ruined the Vineyard, ruined it with reference to that original set of theology and values. The corporate culture we had created, which was a combination of theology and values, was forever altered.

The Kansas City Prophets, according to their critics, adopted the theology of the "Latter Rain" movement, which taught that an outpouring of the Holy Spirit will take place during the End Times right before Jesus' return to earth, which they believe is happening now. Part of this outpouring is that the roles of apostle and prophet will be restored to the church. They believed that local churches should not make major decisions without receiving prophetic direction from proven prophets or apostles.

In 1949 the Assemblies of God made an official resolution condemning the Latter Rain movement, stating that the teaching that the church's foundation is or should be modern-day "apostles and prophets" and an overreliance on direct prophecy from God were "unfounded Scripturally" and "tend to confusion and division among the members of the Body of Christ" (Assemblies of God, 1949). This position was reaffirmed in 2000 when the Assemblies of God denomination made another resolution stating, among other things, that "teaching that present-day offices of apostles and prophets should govern church ministry" is a "departure from Scripture" (Assemblies of God 2000). Indeed, many of the teachings of the Kansas City Prophets seemed to mirror those of the Latter Rain movement, which was heavily criticized among Pentecostal denominations.

The second controversy that emerged from the Vineyard movement in the 1990s was the so-called Toronto Blessing. In 1994, John and Carol Arnott invited Charismatic evangelist Randy Clark to preach at revival meetings at their church, the Toronto Airport Vineyard Church (TAVC). Clark had been influenced by Rodney

Howard-Brown, a South African preacher, whose ministries were known for various manifestations of the Holy Spirit, such as "holy laughter," "falling in the spirit," shaking, and crying. During Clark's time at TAVC, those same manifestations appeared among those attending the revival meetings.

The church began to hold meetings six nights a week for an entire year as people continued to experience physical manifestations such as rolling on the ground, crying, laughing, and sometimes making animal-like noises. News of this "blessing" spread around the world, and people began to visit the TAVC in large numbers. This caused controversy among Vineyard movement leaders, who saw the manifestations as chaotic, extreme, or even demonic. Wimber eventually asked John Arnott to rein in these more extreme practices. Arnott refused, and Wimber decided to disaffiliate TAVC from the Vineyard. Interestingly, Wimber dismissed the Arnotts for similar reasons, and in much the same way, that Chuck Smith had dismissed Wimber in 1982—for experimental practices regarding the Holy Spirit. According to a former leader in the Vineyard,

> We disassociated with [the Toronto Vineyard] because they weren't willing to hold on to our evangelical values, that the Holy Spirit was not given just to have a party and for people to bark and roar and roll on the floor, but the Spirit was given to be a guide, a teacher, to give us gifts, give us character, all for the purpose of continuing the mission of Jesus on the earth. I remember John [Arnott] saying to me, "I desperately have wanted to be filled with the Spirit my whole life, and I made this vow to God that if I ever was, that I would never try to control him." And he was living out of that value system. So anything that happened was OK. And the weirder the better, because the weirder, the thought went, it was the more certain it was probably God, so barking, roaring, rolling on the floor, whatever, it was all seen—and the weirder it got, and it got really weird, that was always a sign to them that it was God.

Despite the official disaffiliation of the TAVC, many within the Vineyard movement continued to visit and be influenced by the Toronto

Blessing. Similarly, many pastors and leaders within the Vineyard continued to be influenced by teachings of the Kansas City Prophets.

A leader in the Vineyard movement stated that after John Wimber died in 1997, he approached some of these controversial leaders in an attempt to get them to make a clear break from their Vineyard ties by starting their own movements with their own names and organizational structures:

> I called [Kansas City Prophet] Mike Bickle and said, "Hey, why don't you take all the Bickle-ites and just sort of go and do your own thing? This is crazy. We can't coexist, our value systems are just completely different." I called John Arnott in Toronto and said, "Why don't you take the Toronto-ites and go do your own thing? It's fine." I wasn't being a hard-ass; I was being genuine. "We can't coexist, we're completely different. Let's just be real. Why don't you take the people who are interested in whatever you're doing, whatever that is, 30, 40, 50, 60 churches, whatever, go do your thing?" So I asked all those guys, literally phoned them and asked them, "Why don't you guys start your own movement and lead it?" And to a man, they all said, "No, we don't want it. We don't want to lead a movement. We don't want to be responsible for churches. We just want to have our voice and do what we do."
>
> So the Vineyard has ended up being a mix. And probably over the last 10 years or so that I've been out of the scene, there have probably been some churches who have left because the Vineyard didn't become Toronto enough, or we've had some churches that have left because the Vineyard became too Toronto. But there was never a mass exodus, and none of those guys ever started a church movement in which they were responsible for church. What they started was more like an affinity network, so people would stay Presbyterian, Lutheran, Methodist, Pentecostal, whatever they were, but they would affiliate based on affinity with Toronto. But they didn't leave their ecclesiastical connections. That I think happened a lot.

This statement articulates what we see as the most important distinction between the third wave neo-Charismatic groups (including Calvary

Chapel, Vineyard, and Hope Chapel) and the new INC Christianity that we describe in this book. As the former Vineyard leader just stated, John Arnott, Mike Bickle, and some of the others who were associated with Vineyard said, "We don't want to lead a movement. We don't want to be responsible for churches." Instead they formed an "affinity network" through which they could focus on building their own personal ministry without having to build an organization consisting of multiple churches. Instead of franchising congregations and building an official "movement" with a particular name, they would instead concentrate on spreading their influence through networks of relationships and media based on new technologies. *It is this shift from "movement" to "network" that we think is most significant in the emergence of INC Christianity.*

Four key leaders who exemplify this shift from organized movement to network all had ties with John Wimber and the Vineyard in the 1980s and 1990s: C. Peter Wagner, Bill Johnson, Che Ahn, and Mike Bickle. We think it is useful to describe the origins of their ministries because they have heavily influenced and exemplify the unique aspects of INC Christianity.

C. PETER WAGNER AND THE WAGNER LEADERSHIP INSTITUTE

C. Peter Wagner, who at this writing has just died at age 86, is a key figure in the rise of INC Christianity. Wagner became a Christian while he was an undergraduate at Rutgers University through interactions with his then-girlfriend and eventual wife, Doris. After they married, they committed themselves to becoming full-time missionaries.

After graduating at Rutgers, Wagner enrolled at Fuller Theological Seminary in Pasadena, California. After receiving a master's degree, he and Doris spent fifteen years as missionaries in Bolivia. In 1971, after earning additional degrees from Princeton Theological Seminary and USC, Wagner accepted a position as professor of Church Growth at his alma mater, Fuller Seminary's School of World Missions. During this period, Wagner described himself as a "cessasionist," meaning he was convinced that miraculous manifestations of the Holy Spirit did not exist and that they had "ceased" after the generation of the original twelve apostles of Jesus.

Wagner became more interested in and open to Pentecostal Christianity when he realized, as a church growth professor who had spent fifteen years in Latin America, that Pentecostalism was the fastest-growing segment of Christianity in that region. In his first book as a Fuller professor—*Look Out! The Pentecostals Are Coming*—he argued that Pentecostals in Latin America were using church growth principles that were superior to those of other Protestant groups.

Wagner's "conversion" to Pentecostal/Charismatic Christianity occurred through his contact with John Wimber. In the early 1970s, Wimber enrolled in one of Wagner's church growth classes at Fuller. At the time, Wimber was pastoring the fast-growing Yorba Linda Friends Church. Wagner was impressed by Wimber's church growth acumen and in 1974 hired him to co-lead the Charles E. Fuller Institute of Evangelism and Church Growth. Wimber left Fuller in 1978 to start what was to become the Anaheim Vineyard. During this time Wagner admired Pentecostal/Charismatic Christianity's growth potential, but was not a practicing Pentecostal/Charismatic Christian himself.

As previously mentioned, in 1982 Wagner invited Wimber to team-teach the Signs, Wonders and Church Growth class at Fuller. Wagner attended the sessions and was the "professor of record" for the class, but Wimber led all of the class activities. In one of the class sessions, Wagner claims he was healed from high blood pressure through Wimber's prayer for him. In his autobiography (2010), Wagner describes the class session:

> When the clinic began, John [Wimber] simply started off by saying, "Who needs healing?" Without any premeditation, I suddenly found my hand in the air! So John said, "Peter, come up here," and he had me sit on a stool facing the class. I told him and the class that I had been diagnosed with high blood pressure for two years and that the doctor had put me on three medications to control it. When John started praying, I felt a warm blanket of power come over me and I felt like my mind

was partially disconnected. I could hear most of what was going on, but I didn't care. To describe it in words that I learned later, I now know that I was slain in the Spirit, but I didn't fall, because I was on the stool.

In keeping with the classroom setting, Wimber brought his students' attention to the telltale signs of the healing process at work:

John was describing my physical reactions to the class like a sports announcer giving a play-by-play account of what was happening to me. "See the eyelids fluttering?" "There's some flushing on the sides of his face!" "Watch the lips—they're quivering!" "Thank You Lord! More power!" A few days later, I went back to the doctor and he took me off of one of the medications. Soon afterward, he took me off the second, and then the third. My blood pressure was fine. This was a turning point. From then on, instead of inspecting what other people were doing, I started praying for the sick as well. I found myself "doin' the stuff!" By the time the course was over, I was no longer a spectator; I was a participant. And I have been a participant ever since (Wagner 2010:130–131).

Both Wagner and Fuller anthropologist Chuck Kraft became disciples of Wimber through the class and continued to promote the miraculous manifestations of the Holy Spirit in their Fuller classes. The Signs, Wonders and Church Growth class, however, was canceled in 1985 as a result of growing criticism from Fuller's theology faculty. The focus of their classes, as was the case in The Signs and Wonders class, was learning to pray for healing and for deliverance from demonic forces.

Wagner began to hold conferences and write books about how the manifestations of the Holy Spirit can result in evangelistic success and church growth—so-called power evangelism, a term coined by Wimber. In 1989 at a National Day of Prayer conference in Washington, DC, he met Cindy Jacobs, the leader of a Charismatic national prayer network and a recognized prophet.

Jacobs introduced Wagner to the idea of praying not only for the healing and deliverance of individuals from demonic forces but for cities and nations as well. This led Wagner to explore the possibility that certain nations and populations that are resistant to Christianity may be under the influence of national or "territorial" demonic forces (Wagner 2010).

Later in 1989 Wagner participated in the Lausanne Congress on World Evangelization in Manila, which brought together evangelicals from all over the world to strategize about how to evangelize globally. Wagner helped organize three "tracks" of sessions: the Holy Spirit Track, the Spiritual Warfare Track, and the Prayer Track. In his presentation to the Spiritual Warfare Track, Wagner promoted the need to wage spiritual warfare against "territorial spirits" that keep people in bondage to various diseases and practices and also keep them resistant to the Christian faith. This conference then led to the convening of high-profile Charismatic leaders to form what became known as the "Spiritual Warfare Network," which included, among others, Cindy Jacobs; John Dawson, president of Youth With a Mission (YWAM); Jack Hayford, former president of the Foursquare denomination (International Church of the Foursquare Gospel); Argentinean evangelist Ed Silvoso; and George Otis, Jr., of the Sentinel Group and creator of the "Transformations" documentaries (Wagner 2010).

The Spiritual Warfare Network developed the concept of "strategic-level spiritual warfare (SLSW)," which we discuss in Chapter 4. Wagner started Global Harvest Ministries in 1991 to focus his efforts on spiritual warfare and was asked by Luis Bush to lead the Prayer Track in the A.D. 2000 movement, which was an evangelical organization dedicated to evangelizing the world by the year 2000.

Wagner's emphasis on SLSW created intensified opposition to Wagner among theologians at Fuller. He also parted ways with John Wimber, who disagreed with the concept of warfare with territorial demons. Wimber was no longer invited to speak as a guest lecturer in Wagner's classes as a result of the split (Wagner 2010).

In 1993, during an A.D. 2000 meeting of leaders in Colorado Springs, Peter and Doris met with Ted Haggard, neo-Charismatic pastor of a local megachurch called the New Life Church. Haggard had long desired to create a "World Prayer Center" in Colorado Springs that would pray strategically for world evangelization on a 24/7 basis. Haggard pitched the idea to Wagner that joining forces and building the World Prayer Center together would benefit their shared vision of praying for the world to·be saved. In 1996 the Wagners made the move to Colorado and, along with Haggard, built the World Prayer Center on the campus of New Life Church.

In 1998, Wagner hired Chuck Pierce, ministry partner of Cindy Jacobs, to run the World Prayer Center and Global Harvest Ministries. Pierce and Wagner then founded the Wagner Leadership Institute (WLI), which he used as a platform to train leaders. The partnership with Haggard lasted until Haggard's highly publicized sex and drug scandal involving a male prostitute (Wagner 2010).

During this period, beginning in the late 1990s, Wagner began to explore the idea that the growth of Pentecostal/Charismatic churches globally was due not only to accessing the power of the Holy Spirit, but also because of the way they were governed. Wagner notes that the leaders of these churches and organizations were strong, independent, and entrepreneurial people who were not governed by boards or denominational structures. He began to theorize about "apostolic" leadership, which meant that those with charismatic authority (in the Weberian sense) were being given the freedom to innovate and lead without organizational constraint in many neo-Charismatic churches. Wagner then coined the term "New Apostolic Reformation" (NAR) to describe this shift from denominational to apostolic leadership in the neo-Charismatic movement worldwide, which he saw as a religio-cultural shift as dramatic as that of the Protestant reformation.

As a result of this new focus, Wagner began to develop relationships with leaders whom he saw as apostles and formed two "apostolic networks": Eagles Vision Apostolic Team (EVAT) and the International Coalition of Apostles (ICA). Wagner until recently led EVAT, which has twenty-five members and provided Wagner with his primary salary in exchange for "apostolic alignment" with him. They met officially once a year, then informally at other times. These apostolic leaders of ministries and organizations thus saw their alliance with Wagner as beneficial, both in terms of networking and as a source of power and authority under God to do their work effectively.

The ICA is a larger group of 400 apostles who also meet annually and pay dues. Recently at age 84, Wagner had given leadership of the WLI to Che Ahn. He handed off leadership of the ICA to apostle John Kelly, and Chuck Pierce leads Global Harvest Ministries, which is now called Global Spheres International.

The WLI is perhaps the largest and best-organized promoter of INC teachings. It describes itself as an "international network of apostolic training centers." The WLI has thirty-nine training centers in fourteen nations and enrolls thousands of students. The WLI offers unaccredited bachelor's, master's, and doctoral degrees in practical ministry. Each diploma requires 120 units of coursework, which can be pursued online as well as through sessions at regional training centers. Courses emphasize prophecy, apostolic leadership, evangelism, and social transformation and are taught by high-profile INC leaders such as Che Ahn, Bill Johnson, Chuck Pierce, Randy Clark, and Cindy Jacobs.

Wagner and his apostles teach that the kingdom of God can and will be founded on earth through the rise of apostles who will establish themselves as leaders in the "Seven Mountains of Culture": religion, education, family, media, arts and entertainment, and business. They also assert that Christian believers will soon be the recipients of "the largest transfer of wealth in the history of mankind," which they will use to bring about the transformation of the world.

Wagner is significant to INC Christianity because he 1) developed the theories and techniques of SLSW, which have been adopted by many INC leaders, 2) developed theories of social transformation that have been adopted by many INC leaders, and 3) theorized and facilitated the creation of networks of apostolic leaders to form cooperative alliances and fundraising networks.

CHE AHN AND HARVEST INTERNATIONAL MINISTRIES

Che Ahn, a Korean American from the East Coast, converted to Christianity through the Calvary Chapel/Jesus movement of the 1970s. He was pastoring a neo-Charismatic church in Maryland in the 1980s when he moved to Pasadena to attend Fuller Seminary. During his time at Fuller, he enrolled in Wimber's and Wagner's Signs, Wonders and Church Growth class.

In 1994, Ahn attended a meeting at the Anaheim Vineyard, led by Wimber, and was touched by the Holy Spirit. According to Ahn, "The Lord impressed upon me to start a church" in Pasadena, which started out as a prayer meeting and grew quickly to a congregation of 300 people. Ahn invited Wimber to speak at his new church. Wimber sensed the Spirit moving there and pitched Che on the idea of having his church join the Vineyard movement.

Che signed on with Wimber because his new church was looking for "covering"—a concept we heard repeatedly—meaning the status of being under the authority of an apostolic leader anointed by God. At the time, Wimber had a vision to plant 300 churches in Asia, but had nobody from an Asian background on the team, so he felt that Che would be a key person to lead this effort.

During that year, 1994, the Toronto Blessing was in full swing at the Airport Vineyard in Toronto, which Ahn and others in his circle had visited. Beginning in April 1995, Ahn's church began to experience a similar "visitation" of the Holy Spirit, including the same visible manifestations such as laughing, crying, shaking, and falling in the Sprit. Like the Toronto Blessing, Ahn's group began to hold nightly meetings.

In 1995, two days after John Wimber disaffiliated from John Arnott's TAVC, Wimber asked Che Ahn either to stop his Toronto-influenced nightly revival meetings or leave the Vineyard movement. Ahn chose to leave the Vineyard a mere nine months after joining. Soon after, Cindy Jacobs approached Che with a word from God that he should start a network of churches. Che believed this was God speaking to him, and ten months later he launched Harvest International Ministries (HIM), in October of 1996.

The goal of HIM was never to build a megachurch; rather, it was to dispatch people around the world to plant new churches. However, Che did not seek to build a movement of affiliated churches. Instead, he sought to build a network of leaders and to empower them in turn to build their own network. According to Ahn,

> We began to realize, "Okay, if I did this full-time, if I was really, really energetic and aggressive, maybe I could oversee a hundred churches, maybe, to do a really good job overseeing them. But if I just became a leader of different leaders, became a network of networks and empowered these other movements to do it and help finance it and raise some funds for it, then there's no limit what you can do." So the Lord gave me that revelation early on, not to just oversee, but to empower other church planters. So we started to grow very rapidly with that concept, and now we have over 8,000 churches and ministries in 42 nations.

Che thus sees himself as an apostle rather than as a pastor, church planter, or missionary. He does not technically "oversee" these 8,000 churches, but they are nonetheless under his apostolic "covering." Chapter 3 describes in more detail how these networks operate.

Essentially Che oversees a small group of apostles, each of whom oversees another group of leaders, pastors, and other apostles, who then oversee others in a multilevel, pyramid-like network. Che has little direct contact with most of the 8,000 churches in his network. He influences them through the network of apostles of which he is the head, and they submit to his apostolic covering by using his leadership resources, attending his conferences, and sending him financial contributions. According to Che, the role of the apostle is to provide the vision to bring the kingdom of heaven to earth. However, he is not involved in any day-to-day work or oversight of individual churches in the network.

Over the years Ahn maintained his relationship with C. Peter Wagner, his former Fuller professor and, as previously mentioned, now has been given leadership over the WLI in Pasadena.

BILL JOHNSON AND BETHEL

Bill Johnson is a fifth-generation pastor whose father was the pastor of Bethel Assemblies of God Church in Redding, California, from 1968 to 1982. Johnson went on staff at his father's church for five years in the 1970s, after which he was commissioned to lead a small Assemblies of God church of forty people in the nearby mountain town of Weaverville, California. After he arrived, the small church quickly grew to 300 members, and he stayed there for seventeen years as head pastor. During that time in Weaverville, Johnson spent a full year focusing his teaching on the "gifts of the Spirit." He would teach on Sunday morning on passages in the Bible in which supernatural miracles occurred; then on Sunday nights the congregation would pray to heal the sick and deliver people from evil spirits and also ask God to reveal things to them through a direct prophetic word. During that year, according to one of the leaders we interviewed, experiences of healing and the supernatural were few and far between.

All of this changed when Johnson and seven other elders and their spouses attended a Vineyard leadership conference at the Anaheim Vineyard. According to one of the leaders present at that time, Johnson came back discouraged because he expected to learn a new way of pursuing the supernatural, but found that John Wimber was teaching the exact same things that Johnson had been teaching for years. The difference was that Wimber was actually getting the miraculous results that were absent at Johnson's church. But during the next service, after the leaders returned had from the conference, "visitations of the Spirit" began to take place at the Weaverville church. One Bethel leader we interviewed described it this way:

> They came back from the Anaheim Vineyard meeting on a Saturday. That very next Sunday we were doing what we always do, people would come up for prayer, we're all praying for people, whatever they wanted, and everybody who went to the Wimber [conference], which was everybody but me, all of their people were falling down under the slaying in the Spirit.... And then people started getting healed more often.

34

Nothing like now, but we got people healed. We didn't just believe in it; it happened. And the Spirit moved differently. Slaying in the Spirit, I know it's faddish, but it just happened. It was kind of cool, like, wow, the person actually experienced God in some way.

The church continued to experience more of the miraculous after that visit to Wimber's leadership conference. Another turning point in Johnson's ministry came when he and his wife, Bennie, visited the Toronto Airport Vineyard in 1994, during the Toronto Blessing. According to one Bethel leader we interviewed,

Bill got radically, radically altered. Under the power of God he saw things there we had never taught, we had never heard about—people falling down in the power, shaking uncontrollably, weeping, crying. It was crazy. So he shared a little bit about Toronto and his experience. It was very casual. I don't remember him actually teaching a lot about it in the beginning. But people began to fall down and shake while he's preaching. Without him doing anything.

My wife, who's the most conservative, nonemotional person, she led worship and I remember this, it was the first couple Sundays [after the Toronto visit], she fell over the keyboards onto the keys, and Bill had to reach over and turn the keyboard off. We had to carry her out to the car and she did that for two or three months. . . . My wife is very conservative, a nonemotional person. And she would just go in our house and fall on the floor and lay there and laugh. Bill would be doing a teaching and people would just spontaneously break out in laughter for things that weren't funny. And the laughter would get so intense that they would fall on the floor.

These Toronto-Blessing–like visitations of the Spirit continued and also brought healings, prophecies from God, and deliverances from evil spirits among the congregation.

In 1996 the "mother" church, Bethel in Redding, was looking for a new pastor (Johnson's father had left fourteen years earlier, and the latest pastor had just departed). Some of the leaders of Bethel desired to see the kinds of miracles that were happening at the church in Weaverville, so they offered the job to Bill. Not all the members of Bethel, however, were thrilled with the new emphasis on the more extreme Toronto-influenced manifestations of the Spirit, and as a result roughly half of the 2,000-member congregation left. At that time, Johnson disaffiliated from the Assemblies of God, feeling that he could not pursue what God was calling him to under that denominational structure.

Two years later, another turning point came when Johnson asked Kris Vallaton, one of the elders working with him in Weaverville, to move to Redding to start the Bethel School of Supernatural Ministry (BSSM). This became a key turning point in transforming Bethel from a fast-growing but isolated congregation to a faster-growing node in an international network. The school was founded on the idea that learning to do supernatural ministry has to be a hands-on, experiential process. Classes include practical courses on how to pray for healing, how to deliver someone from a demonic presence, and how to receive prophetic words directly from God. BSSM students regularly go out into the Redding community and practice these techniques in shopping centers, parks, and other public places. Students enroll initially for a one-year program. If they show promise and maturity, they are asked to complete a second year. Only a small number are asked to complete a third year, which is a yearlong ministry internship for those who are being groomed for leadership.

The BSSM began in 1998 with 37 students. The next year it enrolled 68. The following year 128 enrolled, and the year after that more than 200 enrolled. BSSM currently has nearly 2,000 students, with over 700 from outside the United States. According to BSSM leaders, Bethel is the largest vocational (non-degree-granting) postsecondary school for international students in the United States. The BSSM transformed the Redding Bethel congregation into a megachurch of more than 5,000 members (BSSM students and their families attend Bethel on Sundays) and nurtured the creation of an international network of like-minded congregations.

Much like Che Ahn, Johnson is not interested in building a denomination or "movement." He is no longer the pastor of Bethel in Redding; his son now is the head pastor. Like Ahn, Johnson spends most of his time doing apostolic work, spreading his influence and vision by speaking at conferences and meeting with other apostles and pastors. He travels 125 days a year, often teaming with members of the "Revival Alliance," which includes INC apostles Georgian and Winnie Banov, Che Ahn, Randy Clark, Heidi Baker, and John Arnott. All of these leaders, or apostles, are influential in the network and provide apostolic covering over numerous churches and ministries, but do not directly oversee them. As we will see in Chapter 3, much of their support and funding comes from outside of their local congregation.

MIKE BICKLE AND THE INTERNATIONAL HOUSE OF PRAYER

Mike Bickle, now in his late 50s, is the son of a professional boxer who traveled internationally. As a result, Bickle grew up around boxing and other professional sports. He had little exposure to the Christian faith until, at age 15, he was invited to a Fellowship of Christian Athletes camp. There he heard former Dallas Cowboys quarterback Roger Staubach give his "testimony" about how God had changed his life, and Bickle decided, "I want what that guy has . . . that's what I want to do with my life."

Soon after his conversion, Bickle joined a Presbyterian church that had a strong Campus Crusade for Christ influence (the pastor was a disciple of Campus Crusade founder Bill Bright). In his 20s, Bickle decided to go into full-time ministry. After a stint at a church in St. Louis, at age 27 he started his own independent, nondenominational evangelical church, Metro Christian Fellowship, in the upscale Overland Park suburb of Kansas City. The church quickly grew to 500 members, which included professionals, business people, and ten players from the Kansas City Chiefs football team. Bickle says that during that time he was actively anti-Charismatic, thinking that an emphasis on the gifts of the Spirit led to deceptions. This all changed when he met a man named Bob Jones, one of the so-called "Kansas City Prophets."

In 1983, when Bickle had only been pastoring his church for a few months, a man approached him and insisted that Bickle meet with the prophet Bob Jones. Bickle dismissed this man numerous times, but the man was persistent, and Bickle finally agreed to meet with Jones. According to Bickle, Jones gave him a prophecy that Bickle would "lead a youth movement that has a global dimension to it of singers and musicians." He went on to say that "the group you're going to touch the most are going to be Asians." Jones then told Bickle, "I saw unplugged TV sets in their hands, all over Asia, in the rice paddies, watching singers and musicians in Grandview."

Bickle said that at the time he simply dismissed Jones's prophecy as "crazy talk." First, Bickle had no intention of moving from upscale Overland Park to Grandview, a working-class suburb of Kansas City. Second, it seemed implausible that his greatest impact would be on Asians if the ministry were located in Grandview, Missouri. Bickle now believes, however, that Jones revealed to him a true vision from God: Bickle's ministry is now located in Grandview, and hundreds of millions of Asians now see the live stream of IHOP worship and prayer sessions on their smart phones, which did not exist in 1983 when Jones gave Bickle this prophecy.

Still, at the time Bickle dismissed Jones's prophecy as bizarre and unlikely, but began praying with his congregation of 500 for revival. They decided to hold prayer meetings at the church every day from 6 am to midnight, and throughout the day different people would come and pray. One day, during those prayer meetings, Bickle felt that God had put a Bible verse, Psalms 27:4, in his head. Bickle kept repeating the verse throughout the day. Bob Jones appeared at the church that day and told him, "The Lord visited me in a dream last night. The Lord said yes to your prayer. He's going to answer your prayer."

Bickle asked Jones what he was talking about, and Jones said, "The one He gave you from Psalm 27:4."

Bickle was shocked that Jones knew the verse that he had been repeating to himself all day. Jones went on to say that some day Bickle would "have 24/7 prayer in the spirit of the tabernacle of David, with singers and musicians." At that point Bickle began to take Jones's prophecies seriously—so much so that he placed a sign in his church that read "Twenty-four hour prayer in the spirit of the tabernacle of David."

One year later, Bickle met with Bob Jones again, and Jones told him, "You're going to interact with a movement 35 miles southeast of LA...I saw a banner over them, Compassion and Worship. Those will be the two things it'll really be connected to, compassion and worship." Bickle again dismissed Jones's "prophecy." Six months later, Bickle traveled to the Anaheim Vineyard to a conference led by John Wimber. Wimber kicked off the conference saying, "Our two main things are compassion and worship." Bickle then remembered Jones's prophecy and began to pay attention. Because of his experiences at the Anaheim Vineyard conference, Bickle began to pursue the gifts of the Spirit, including prophecy, healing, and deliverance from evil spirits.

After his visit to Anaheim Vineyard, Bickle began to meet with Jones regularly and to take his prophecies much more seriously. Four years later, in 1987, Jones told Bickle that God revealed to him in a dream that in 1988 John Wimber would call him. In January of 1988, Wimber did call Bickle to say that he wanted him to come to Anaheim for a meeting. Bickle felt that this was a sign from God and went to Anaheim the next week.

Bickle and Wimber connected strongly, and Bickle began to travel with Wimber to speak at conferences. As a former Vineyard leader previously stated, this association caused controversy within the Vineyard movement. Some thought that Bickle and his association with Bob Jones and the Kansas City Prophets would lead the Vineyard down the path of extremism, particularly concerning outrageous claims in the area of prophecy.

For three years, Bickle and Wimber led two or three conferences per month all over the world emphasizing the gifts of the Spirit. During this period, Bickle and other Kansas City Prophets—including Bob Jones, Paul Cain, and John Paul Jackson—participated in these events, promoting the importance of prophecy. The Vineyard leaders we spoke to who were there at that time admitted that these prophets had an uncanny ability to know and predict events in people's lives through visions and "words from the Lord." They also said that these leaders often "overreached" and began to offer predictions involving world events that, according to one leader, "were almost always wrong." It was these more extreme attempts at prophecy, along with a lack of emphasis on and understanding of evangelical theology, that made Vineyard leaders nervous. Eventually, Bickle and the other Kansas City Prophets became frustrated with the Vineyard for its lack of enthusiasm, and sometimes outright skepticism of their style of prophecy, causing them eventually to stop speaking at Vineyard-sponsored conferences.

After the break with the Vineyard, Bickle started a 24/7 prayer movement, as predicted by Bob Jones, "in the spirit of the tabernacle of David, with singers and musicians," which was to become IHOP. He also left the Metro Christian Fellowship in order to start Forerunner Christian Fellowship, the church of which he currently is the head pastor and that currently has 5,000 attendees each Sunday. After Wimber's death in 1997, the new Vineyard leadership disassociated themselves completely from Bickle and the Kansas City Prophets.

IHOP now consists of several locations and ministries in metro Kansas City. Its central facility is a former strip mall in Grandview that contains a 24/7 prayer room, healing room, prophecy room, and bookstore–coffee shop. IHOP's City of Hope, near downtown Kansas City, consists of a prayer room, soup kitchen, and two dorms for homeless people. IHOPU, a nonaccredited Bible college in another converted strip mall a few miles away from the central facility in Grandview, enrolls 700 full-time students. In all, there are 1,000 staff members (700 full time) and 3,000 interns who must raise their own financial support to work at IHOP.

Like Bethel and HIM, Mike Bickle and the IHOP leadership do not want to create a movement, denomination, or association of churches. They simply want to run their own center and influence others through the people they dispatch from their programs in Kansas City, as well as through their live-streaming prayer room. According to a senior leader of IHOP,

> One of our key public commitments, it's the thing we said for 14 years that we'll never undo, is that we will never start another IHOP. We will never, ever start one, meaning, we've had hundreds of people get trained and leave, but they have to start something that joins their own ministry in another city. They can be our friend, but they can't join us. So when they go, they join many mainline churches, many Charismatic, nondenominational churches, college campus ministries. They have to join someone else when they leave us. Or they could start something new if they want, but they can't be IHOP. Our real reason why is, we just don't want to govern other things. We want to inspire, not govern.
>
> The goal of IHOP is simply to influence other churches and ministries to pray more.

They believe that this will bring revival to the world and hasten the time when Jesus will come back to earth to finish the redemption of the planet. According to another leader within IHOP,

> One of my real big points is not to measure, which is almost opposite of growth paradigms. Normally you set a goal that is measurable. We don't have goals. Our goal is to inspire and just throw it to the wind and see what happens. We don't have a goal of how many will do it and who we'll be connected to. That takes a lot of the pressure off. We don't have any goals, just to inspire people and send them to their home, to their cities, go do what you do and see what happens.

Similar to those of Bethel and HIM, IHOP's leaders decided that they could expand their influence more effectively through networks of individuals sent out from their base rather than through building institutions and formal organizations.

There are a number of similarities that tie these four INC leaders and their ministries together. Using the conceptual categories of the

"religious economy" paradigm, they have 1) organizational structures, 2) products, and 3) marketing and funding techniques that are
quite different from the "new paradigm" neo-Charismatic groups that
Miller (1997) described, as well as from other traditionally organized
religious groups.

First, their organizational structures are quite different. INC
Christianity is organized as a network of influential leaders rather
than as a movement consisting of multiple congregations, as is the case
with the third wave neo-Charismatic movements. Second, the product
they are promoting is not primarily the ability to access supernatural
power to gain converts and build congregations, but, more important,
to participate in the establishment of God's kingdom on earth in the
here and now.

Previous iterations of neo-Charismatic Christianity had as their
goal the expansion of the church through revival and conversion of
nonbelievers. Depending on the leader, the product INC Christianity
is selling is either participation in hastening the return of Jesus to
establish His rule on earth or actually becoming the agents of God's
rule on earth. Thus the benefits that the product promises to the consumer have risen considerably over previous iterations of Pentecostal/
Charismatic Christianity.

Finally, INC Christianity is marketed primarily through electronic
media rather than through the long-term project of building congregations. We think that these differences are important enough to allow
us characterize INC Christianity as fundamentally different from the
third wave neo-Charismatic new paradigm movements from which
they emerged. We also think that INC Christianity has significant
competitive advantages over other types of Christianity, including new
paradigm neo-Charismatic Christianity that will enable it to continue
to gain market share in the future.

THEORIZING THE EMERGENCE OF INC CHRISTIANITY

How are we to understand the rise of this phenomenon? Social theory
can greatly help. One approach is to identify the patterns of routinization

in religious groups first identified by Max Weber. According to Weber, the charismatic authority of leaders derives from the personal devotion of their followers, which is typically inspired by the extraordinary ability of the leaders to perform miracles or heroic acts (Weber 1978). It is these acts that give followers the sense that the leader has been chosen or is a special recipient of God's grace (Weber 1978:140). Weber states that charisma is "guaranteed by what is held to be a proof, originally always a miracle" (Weber 1978:242). The charismatic leader "gains and retains it solely by proving his powers in practice. He must work miracles, if he wants to be a prophet" (Weber 1978:1114).

Weber contrasts this form of authority with traditional or rational–legal authority. He states,

> In radical contrast to bureaucratic organization, charisma knows no formal and regulated appointment or dismissal, no career, advancement or salary, no supervisory or appeals body, no local or purely technical jurisdiction, and no permanent institutions in the manner of bureaucratic agencies (Weber 1978:1112).

The charismatic form of authority has been the stock-in-trade of the Pentecostal movement throughout its history. Strong, charismatic leaders able to perform miracles through the power of the Holy Spirit continually emerge to start new movements. As these movements grow they inevitably become too large for the charismatic leader to manage, and the transition to a more rational, bureaucratic organization emerges.

This development then leads to attempts to routinize and replicate the miraculous practices of the original leader. Those leaders in charge of managing the organization rarely can replicate the miraculous and heroic acts of the original leader, and the movement therefore transitions into what Weber terms rational–legal authority. At this point the charismatic leader is replaced by the organization he or she leaves in his or her wake, and denominations and other formal organizations carry on the work of the original leader, without the charisma. As a result, the organization can maintain the work of the charismatic originator, but the lack of charisma makes drawing new followers increasingly difficult over time (see Miller 1997; Poloma 1989).

Inevitably another leader endowed with charisma arises within or from outside of these organizations, performing heroic acts or miracles and offering new ways to experience the supernatural, and the process repeats itself. Weber states that charisma "cannot remain stable, but becomes either traditionalized or rationalized, or a combination of both" (Weber 1978:244). This is what Weber termed the "routinization of charisma," which he believed was inevitable under the rationalization process of modernity.

From this perspective, one could interpret the emergence of INC Christianity as simply another round in the routinization "product cycle." The first wave of Pentecostalism eventually routinized into denominations, while the postwar Charismatic renewal attempted to bring Charismatic practices into established denominations, with varying degrees of success. Third wave neo-Charismatic leaders such as Chuck Smith, Lonnie Frisbee, and John Wimber broke the constraints of denominational Christianity through the sheer force of their personalities, and their ability to access the supernatural allowed them to inspire their own movements.

These movements, as they grew, became too large for the founding leader to manage, and controversies emerged that forced them to standardize and routinize their charisma. As Calvary Chapel and Vineyard became more cautious and began to exert organizational control over controversial practices, new leaders with charismatic authority emerged and broke off from established groups to found their own ministries. Routinization theory would therefore predict that as INC ministries get too large and as their leaders age, they will eventually routinize their ministries by creating formal bureaucracies to manage growth and exercise control over controversial practices.

Time will tell whether groups like HIM, Bethel, and IHOP will indeed come to resemble formal denominations as they continue to grow and as their founders are forced to pass the mantle to younger leaders. These leaders insist, however, that they are committed to never

44

formalizing their growing ministries into denominational structures. They all say that they do not want to start a movement and refuse to let spin-off churches and ministries use their name. Another way to look at the emergence of INC Christianity is to see it as an alternative mode of organizing religious practice, one that is based on networks of individual leaders rather than on formal organizations.

Rather than seeing the emergence of INC Christianity as simply another round in the Weberian routinization process, one could see its emergence as part of a larger societal shift away from formal organizations toward networks as the primary organizing matrix of social groups (see, for example, Castells 2000;2004 Van Dijk 2006). Analysts of global capitalism have been making this claim for some time (see Powell 1990; Uzzi 1996; Gereffi 1996 Jones et al. 1997).

In the last two or three decades, the advent of digital communications technologies has created new ways of organizing people around a common goal. The ability of people and groups to communicate easily and quickly over great distances has increased the capacity of networks to mobilize people and resources while still retaining their inherent flexibility and adaptability (Castells and Cardoso 2005).

Thus coordination of a large, decentralized global network of actors outside a formal organization to complete a task is now possible. It could be that INC leaders have simply realized that they have more freedom, flexibility, and lower overhead by organizing themselves into networks rather than by building formal organizations. They can maximize their influence and minimize their costs by going directly to the "consumer" with their "product" rather than delivering the product through a formal congregation or denomination.

A number of scholars have noticed this recent shift toward network governance among fast-growing Pentecostal groups. Miller and Yamamori (2007), in their sweeping analysis of global Pentecostalism, note, "Many of the most progressive Pentecostal churches are not part of a formal denomination. Instead, they tend to associate with networks of like-minded church leaders" (p. 207).

45

Similarly, Flory and Sargeant (2013), in their explanation for the rapid growth of Pentecostalism around the world, state that although there are some large churches and organizations within Pentecostalism that have a top-down organizational authority structure, most of the growth is among independent groups led by individual religious entrepreneurs who are willing to take risks and who operate best where formal bureaucracy is absent. This allows innovative charismatic leaders to move quickly into opportunities in the religious marketplace that are not being exploited. "There is no need to go through a bureaucracy or find a seminary-trained minister; instead, they simply find a place to meet, create a new identity, and start off on their own" (Flory and Sargeant 2013; 305).

Kay (2007) documents the emergence of apostolic networks in Britain, which he describes as "centered around the guiding ministry of an apostle" operating outside of traditional denominations (p. 20). According to Kay, "There are no time honored procedures or traditions. Nor is there a bureaucratic or legal basis for the network; everything is vested in the apostle and the charismata of the apostle" (p. 20). Kay concludes that these networks will continue to grow while traditional denominations decline and speculates that these networks may ultimately replace institutions and alter the religious landscape, giving new life and an energized capacity for the expansion of Charismatic/Pentecostal Christianity (p. 353).

In observing current networks of Pentecostal leaders, Lord (2012) makes the case that network structures have always been particularly well suited to Pentecostal theology and practice, particularly where "movements of leaders" are led by the Spirit to connect and collaborate in a mission to expand their following outside of formal organizations. Lord's theological–ecclesiastical work links the emergence of networks to the distinctive beliefs and practices of Pentecostalism throughout history.

Thus there are a growing number of scholars who are seeing the phenomenon we describe here—the emergence of networks of dynamic individual leaders as a common feature of many of the fastest growing

Pentecostal/Charismatic groups around the world. None of these scholars, however, analyzes this form of governance from an in-depth sociological perspective, demonstrating the competitive advantages of network governance in the current religious marketplace. We now turn to that task.

CHAPTER THREE

INNOVATIONS
IN GOVERNANCE

NETWORKS AND APOSTLES

Early in the morning on April 9, 2016, Lou Engle, founder and leader of The Call, an INC intercessory prayer ministry, addresses the small but growing crowd at the Los Angeles Memorial Coliseum, kicking off the sixteen-hour INC-organized event named "Azusa Now" (a reference to the Azusa Street Revival in 1906 credited with starting the Pentecostal movement): "the skies are open...Lord we invoke your presence in this stadium, we invoke the presence and power of the Holy Spirit worldwide as people watch on GodTV, we invoke your presence as live streaming webcasts are going forward, we say Lord release this shift into a day of your third great awakening in America, we call for the outpourings of the Holy Spirit worldwide."

Eleven hours later, more than 50,000 people erupt in loud cheers and applause as Bill Johnson takes the stage at the stadium and calls out to the crowd:

You can't invite Jesus to a party and then not expect him to do what he does...and I'm expecting that he's going to manifest himself powerfully...in the great commission he said go into all the world preach the gospel of the kingdom then heal the sick raise the dead, cast out devils, cleanse lepers...He's been doing this all day long and I believe it's about to increase exponentially...people have been getting healed all day...we know of a wheelchair outside that was emptied before even coming in . . . we know of at least one wheelchair that has been emptied since we've come in . . . we've had our teams out on the streets of LA for the past 4, 5 or 6 days they've been seeing blind eyes opened, people born deaf many deaf ears opened, people getting up out of wheelchairs, it's the time of the visitation of God to demonstrate his love to restore broken people and that's you and that's me.

He then calls out to an audience member:

. . . specifically there is someone here who has a metal rod in their right thigh . . . you have restricted movement, pain; there's great difficulty because of that accident, Jesus is going to heal you . . . we have seen numerous cases where the metal is replaced with actual bone. There are a number of people with deaf ears . . . the Lord is opening deaf ears. And I tell you as soon as something significant happens in your body, I want you to go to exit number 6 we have a team of people with red shirt, tell them what Jesus did. Let's give a shout of praise to the Lord for what's about to happen.

After about forty minutes of worship music, Johnson then returns to the stage and calls out to the crowd and prays for the crowd to receive healing power and then says "I want anyone who has any measure of loss of hearing to right now put their hand up . . . we're just going to go for this right off the bat." He then asks people around those with their hands up to pray for the restoration of their hearing. After this, he calls out to those with rheumatoid arthritis to raise their hand and again charges those next to them to pray for healing . . . "to command that affliction to be broken off of them." He then calls people watching on GodTV to pray for healing:

God heals through TV constantly, we constantly get reports of people that experience the power of God in their living room watching on their iPhones and their iPads as God releases the power of the gospel into homes, into automobiles, into places of recreation.

Johnson then gets a "word from the Lord" of a healing taking place at that moment:

> There's an injury to the lower part of the spine it's from the tailbone up to about 3 or 4 inches above the belt line. Jesus is restoring somebody in that part of their body right now. There is numbness, paralysis, God is restoring and bringing life to you right now.

He then asks everyone who has just been healed to wave their hands into the air. The crowd erupts in loud cheers as dozens of people wave their hands over their heads.

The headline speakers of the conference—Lou Engle, Bill Johnson, Heidi Baker, Cindy Jacobs, Che Ahn, Georgian Banov, Dutch Sheets, Todd White, and Daniel Kolenda regularly appear together at conferences all over the world. They each not only lead their own churches and ministries but also provide "apostolic covering" for a network of other churches and ministries that they do not supervise. They all have reputations of producing miraculous "signs and wonders."

Christianity Today magazine recently featured Heidi Baker on its cover and detailed her ministry in Mozambique, which includes, according to the magazine article, "credible reports of people raised from the dead" (Stafford 2012).

These leaders epitomize the idea of "apostolic networks" that is essential in INC Christianity. We think that this structure represents an organizational innovation that has the potential to change the way that Christianity is practiced and experienced by significant numbers of people. This chapter documents and attempts to theoretically explain the rise of this new organizational mode of charismatic leadership.

CHARISMA AND APOSTOLIC LEADERSHIP

Max Weber described charisma as

> [A] certain quality of an individual personality, by virtue of which he is set apart from ordinary men and treated as endowed with supernatural,

superhuman, or at least specifically exceptional powers or qualities. These are such as are not accessible to the ordinary person, but are regarded as of divine origin or as exemplary, and on the basis of them the individual concerned is treated as a leader (Weber 1978:241).

The INC leaders we describe in this book all have this Weberian quality of charisma. They are seen by their followers as having supernatural qualities of divine origin and are followed by large numbers of people for this reason. The INC leaders we interviewed are very much aware of Weber's theory of routinization and are actively trying to avoid what Weber saw as an inevitable shift from charismatic authority to rational–legal authority. They believed they have found a way out of the seemingly inevitable routinization process—apostolic networks.

We consistently heard these leaders speak of "apostolic" leadership as being the key to understanding the success of INC Christianity. This was not a term we were initially familiar with, so we searched the leadership literature used by these groups and asked the leaders themselves how they understood "apostolic leadership." Although each offered a slightly different definition and explanation, they all had certain similarities.

Most referred to what they called the "fivefold gifts" of ministry, which is a reference to several instances in the New Testament where the apostle Paul lists five roles in church leadership. Ephesians 4:11 is a common reference that proponents of the idea of apostolic leadership regularly cite: "And He Himself gave some to be apostles, some prophets, some evangelists, and some pastors and teachers" (New International Version).

Over the centuries there has been considerable disagreement among theologians and church leaders over the meaning of the term "apostle" in Paul's writing. The Catholic Church, for example, sees a direct transfer of apostolic leadership from the original twelve apostles to early church leaders, who are now succeeded by the popes of the church. Protestants, however, beginning with Calvin and Luther, tend to view apostles as only the foundational leaders of the early Christian movement, which means they are no longer necessary. Most classical

Pentecostal denominations also reject the role of apostle as having relevance for current church practice. In fact, this return of the offices of apostle was the primary reason the Assemblies of God denomination rejected the "Latter Rain" movement.

Most INC leaders, however, are heavily invested in the idea that the role of apostle continues to be a key element of the Christian movement worldwide. In fact, many believe that neglect of this apostolic leadership has hindered the growth of Christianity in the past and that the rediscovery of the apostle's role is the essential ingredient of a new global revival.

Despite the general agreement over the importance of recovering the role of apostle for the spread of Christianity among INC leaders, there are varying definitions of what an apostle does. However, there is agreement that the apostle has extraordinary leadership abilities backed by supernatural powers, very similar to Weber's idea of charisma.

One popular INC book explained the concept of apostolic leadership in this way:

> Apostles exude authority. Active or dormant, their authority is difficult to disregard. It is the first obvious distinguishing feature. Whatever the situation, the apostle inevitably stands out. He unavoidably finds himself in charge or it is thrust upon him. He competently makes decisions and often casts the deciding vote. Apostles lead when they do not try to, are looked to and relied upon when others seek a strong hand. They command attention and provoke obedience because of God's blatant authority upon them. Extended involvement with an apostle puts you face to face with authority (Price 1994).

C. Peter Wagner also emphasizes the importance of authority in recognizing and apostle:

> While there are several things that distinguish apostles from other members of the Body of Christ, the major characteristic that stands out over the others is their exceptional authority (Wagner 2010).

The common theme in the literature on apostolic leadership is that, like Weber's charismatic figure, apostles "exude authority"—people naturally follow their lead, and their authority is authenticated by their ability to produce miraculous "signs and wonders."

APOSTLES, NETWORKS, AND ROUTINIZATION

New communications technologies such as the Internet as well as the relative ease and affordability of international travel have allowed for the emergence of networks of apostolic leaders around the world who can communicate easily with each other and with followers all over the world. They can also organize events and projects together and share techniques, information, and ideas.

These relational networks of apostles represent a way of organizing religious groups that, according to proponents, avoid the pitfalls of routinization. If leaders with charisma can form a network with each other, then this network can enable the sharing of resources as well as followers, which allows each leader in the network to increase his or her following without having to submit to the authority of an overarching organization with its limiting rules and regulations.

Furthermore, the network is not dependent on any individual leader, so when a charismatic leader dies or retires, the network lives on without having to rely on bureaucratic structures to perpetuate its web of relationships. New leaders with charisma continually join the network, bringing new converts into the fold. Free from the constraints of formal denominations and their bureaucratic structures, including boards, presbyteries, general assemblies, church councils, elder boards, sessions, and vestries, leaders with charisma are free to experiment, innovate, and lead in ways to which they feel the Holy Spirit is calling them. In our study of INC leaders, we identified two main types of networks led by apostles: vertical and horizontal networks.

VERTICAL NETWORKS

The vertical apostolic network is structured like a pyramid, with a head apostle at the top and other apostles below the head apostle. At the next layer are still more apostles, leaders, evangelists, prophets, and business people (see Figure 3.1). Others are "aligned" with the apostle in the broader network to give them "covering," meaning that if someone asks with whom they are associated, they can respond that they are a part of a broader apostles ministry. Being covered also means that if the leader is aligned with a particular apostle, the anointing of the Holy Spirit on that apostle will "trickle down" to him or her.

According to a number of apostles we interviewed, the way they know if someone is genuinely aligned with them is that they contribute money to the person from whom they want covering. To put the matter somewhat crudely, legitimacy and spiritual power flow down from the apostle at the top of the pyramid, and allegiance and money flow up the pyramid.

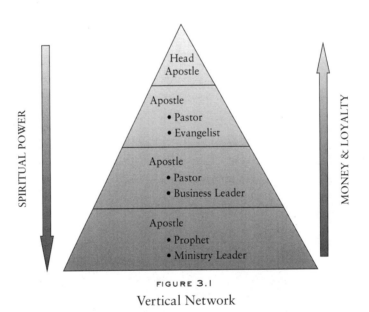

FIGURE 3.1

Vertical Network

An example of a vertical network structure is Harvest International Ministries (HIM), whose head apostle is Che Ahn. Ahn's ministry is not remarkable for the size of his congregation. Although his congregation, called HROCK, is large (1,000 members), its size is not unusual in Southern California, where the largest megachurches have over 20,000 members. What is remarkable is Ahn's large apostolic network, called HIM, which "oversees" about 8,000 churches and ministries in 42 countries. Notable members of this network are Lou Engle—whose ministry, The Call, was a key organizer of Governor Rick Perry's "The Response" prayer rally and the Azusa Now event—and Heidi Baker, who operates a number of large ministries and orphanages in Mozambique.

What does it mean that Ahn, as the head apostle, oversees thousands of churches and ministries across the globe? One partner in Che Ahn's ministry explained Ahn's relationship with Heidi Baker in Africa:

> Interviewer: How is Che involved with her? What does she get out of that relationship? How often do they meet? What does she get from him?
>
> Respondent: What she gets is apostolic alignment. She knows that there's a biblical reason for aligning with an apostle. There are biblical teachings on this. So what Heidi gets out of it is spiritual enhancement of her work, to put it in those terms. What Che gets out of it, Heidi contributes [financially] to Che. However, Che also raises money for projects for Heidi. So in that case, there's a mutual exchange of funds. And what they get out of it is the satisfaction that they're properly aligned in proper government. So Heidi has Che over her, and that gives her security. She has somebody to go to. If somebody asks her, "Who are you? Where do you come from?" she answers, "Che Ahn is my apostle. I belong to HIM, Harvest International Ministries." That's the benefit she gets out of it.

Ahn has never met many or perhaps most of the leaders he oversees. Which raises the question: In what sense is this a governance structure with "teeth" if the head apostle doesn't ever see or meet those underneath him or her on the pyramid? A leader in the Ahn's apostolic network explains:

> There is a clear avoidance of any kind of control or manipulation. There's an avoidance of legal authority over people. We call it all relational. There are 30 or 40 HIM churches in Australia, and Bruce Lindsay is the head of those. [Ahn's] purpose is to help Bruce fulfill the vision that God has given to Bruce. Not to tell Bruce what to do, but to help him. Now, if Bruce says, "Hey, I have this problem here, there's these pastors doing this, I need your help," Che will help him as much as he can. But there isn't an awful lot of that. For apostolic leadership, it's really kind of a smooth government, particularly since it's all voluntary and it's all grateful. Nobody makes them. They don't have to follow that apostle. The reason they follow the apostle is because they're grateful for the value added that they have from following the apostle in whatever they do. But if anything ever happens, if they begin to disagree with the apostle, it's very simple. They find another apostle. So you don't have any legal problems with that, since it's all voluntary and relational.

It appears, from this description, that this form of governance does not involve the kind of accountability and obligation that traditional denominational structures usually entail. Leaders align with apostles for the covering and spiritual power they can bring to the table, and apostles help leaders fulfill their vision the best they can and receive financial support in return. In a vertical network, leaders under the head apostle may rarely, if ever, meet the head apostle personally. Instead they would have direct contact with an apostle lower on the pyramid. Members of a network of apostles are expected to contribute financially to the apostle (although contributions are technically voluntary) and to come to meetings convened by the network, which are typically held once or twice a year. One leader of an apostolic network explained the financial aspect of aligning with an apostle:

The relationship is confirmed and perpetuated by money. People give to the person they follow. Most of these networks, the contributions are voluntary. But we keep track of them, and if people have failed to give for a while, we call it to their attention and ask if they really want to continue to participate or not. The other thing is that you come together. They need to come to conferences like this often enough so that they are recognized as part of [the network].

If there is a disagreement between an apostle and a person under him or her in the vertical network, the pastor or leader may simply find another apostle who is more willing to support his or her goals and methods.

This raises the question of whether an apostle has the authority to remove people from their network if the apostle disagrees with some aspect of the ministry or the behavior of the leader they are overseeing. There do seem to be occasions, although rare, when apostles have removed people from their network because of misconduct. One apostle of a large network explained it this way:

When I ran [my network] for 10 years, we had certain apostles who went off the track, mostly on moral issues. So when that report would come to me, I would have to take action. I would have to fact-find, find out what was going on, follow it as much as I could until I came to a point where I thought I had a grasp to make a decision. And I think in 10 years I dismissed six people from [my network] on the basis of moral concerns.

One of them fell into sin, and it became revealed that he was homosexual. He was in my network. Within 24 hours, the apostle that he was under had gone and visited him, had connected with him to deal with this. He rejected that apostle's advice. That was enough to get him dismissed from [the network]. Then he found another apostle that was a little kinder and more gentle and put himself under that apostle, who was not a member of [my network]. If the other apostle was a member of [my network], I wouldn't have allowed it. I would have found a way to stop that.

This reveals the flexible and contingent nature of governance under an apostolic network. Under a more formal organizational structure, such as a traditional denomination, pastors and leaders are subject to the rules and authority of the organization. If a pastor runs afoul of these rules, he or she may be removed from their position and lose their ability to lead within that denomination. In a network, no such authority exists—apostles are there simply to "add value" or provide "alignment" in the form of legitimacy or spiritual power to the ministry of those under them. If an irreconcilable difference emerges between an apostle and those who are under him or her in the vertical network, the leader may simply find another apostle to align with and move on.

Another revealing example of a vertical apostolic network is Chuck Pierce's Glory of Zion ministries, based in a 200,000-square-foot former Boeing factory in Corinth, Texas (just outside of Dallas), called the Global Spheres Center. Pierce has used the Internet to create one of the most expansive neo-Charismatic networks in the world. His network consists of his megachurch in Corinth as well as individuals, house churches, businesses, and nonprofit organizations, all linked through online media and forums. Pierce is also aligned under the EVAT network formerly of C. Peter Wagner.

Pierce's congregation, Glory of Zion, holds Sunday services at the Global Spheres Center, which includes a sanctuary that can accommodate 2,000 worshippers. Sunday services are broadcast over the Internet. The network also has more than 600 house churches, called Churches of Zion, in which small groups of people meet in their homes, pray together, and watch the webcast of the Glory of Zion Sunday service together. These house churches send their tithes and donations to the organization's main headquarters in Corinth.

Robert Heidler is the main teaching pastor of Glory of Zion Corinth, but it is clear who the apostle is and therefore who is in charge. According to a leader in Pierce's network, "Everybody in the church recognizes [Pierce's] apostolic leadership. And he runs that church. There's no one else that runs that church. He makes all the decisions about what's going to happen, who's going to do what, when, where."

The network also includes 5,000 "Houses of Zion" that are not house churches, but households that want to align themselves with Pierce as their apostle. Sixty-thousand individuals are also connected to Glory of Zion through the organization's e-mail network, through which Pierce sends daily encouragements and prophetic words from God. There are also more than a thousand 501(c)3 nonprofit ministries associated with the network called "Ministries of Zion." These include missionary organizations, prayer ministries, ministries delivering people from demonic influences, and organizations doing social service work.

Interestingly, Pierce's network also contains over a hundred "Businesses of Zion"—small, privately owned businesses that want to be aligned with Chuck Pierce as their apostle. According to a leader in Pierce's network,

> The business leader has a restaurant. They want their restaurant apostolically aligned, so the leader says, "I want my business aligned with you, and because my business is aligned with you, we're going to prosper more in our business than we would if we weren't aligned." They tithe their business money to him.

In reference to Chuck Pierce, one apostolic leader who is part of Pierce's network stated:

> The total number of aligned people on his mailing list is 60,000. But these people send him money, my wife and I send him our tithe, and we're not the only ones. He has all the money he needs. Even for renovating that 215,000 square foot, 31-acre facility. The money just pours in. And he is the only one who decides how to spend that money. That's quite different from the traditional way of governance. And everybody loves it. And everybody keeps sending him money, because they trust the way that the Holy Spirit is leading him to spend their money.

Both HIM and Glory of Zion are paradignmatic example of vertical networks: They are hierarchical and flexible networks in which money and loyalty flows upward and spiritual power and authority flow downward.

HORIZONTAL NETWORKS

In contrast, horizontal apostolic networks are nonhierarchical. In these types of networks, apostles do not expect financial contributions or participation in annual meetings or any of their networks activities. They offer their advice, resources, and material support to those who are interested, but do not establish formal ties or requirements of any kind for those in their network (see Figure 3.2). Leaders and other apostles may want to join a horizontal network for many of the same reasons they would join a vertical network: primarily to gain the perceived spiritual blessings that are flowing to the members of the network.

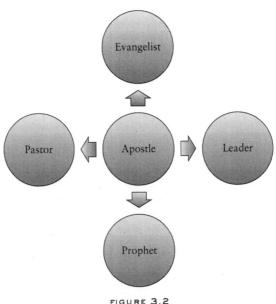

FIGURE 3.2

Horizontal Network

Practically speaking, they can claim to be aligned with the apostle and be part of a group larger than their own ministries. They can also participate in conferences or services that the network provides. However, because a member of a horizontal network is not "under" the authority of an apostle, they may not receive the perceived legitimacy that comes from a vertical network affiliation. The horizontal network member has no financial obligation or other requirements for membership in the network, leaving even more flexibility and freedom within the network.

In 2005, Bill Johnson contacted Paul Manwaring, a top-level executive in Britain's prison system, to come to Bethel in Redding to build an international horizontal network. Manwaring moved to Redding and created the Global Legacy network. Global Legacy consists of revival leaders, pastors, professionals, and anyone else who wants apostolic covering under Bill Johnson and Bethel. What distinguishes Global Legacy from HIM and Glory of Zion is that joining Global Legacy entails no particular expectations or requirements. Anyone can simply go on the Global Legacy website and create a profile (we did this; it was very simple). The Bethel leadership decided that requiring members to donate or to attend meetings was contrary to the "freedom of heaven." According to Manwaring,

> It's not based on rules. You can't be trained for freedom in captivity. I learned that running prisons. You can't be trained for the freedom of heaven in a structure of law. Self-governance is the goal. We build out of honor, freedom and love.

Manwaring read John Wimber's history of the Vineyard and decided that trying to routinize revival will only kill the Spirit. The challenge, he says, is denominationalism. Ordination requirements, doctrinal statements, and other rules create a bureaucracy in which the purpose inevitably becomes serving the bureaucracy instead of the original vision.

Besides providing "apostolic alignment" and the resulting blessings from God, Global Legacy provides access to its website, which allows members to identify other members in any location and connect with them. They also hold videoconferences, provide a distance-learning leadership development course, and organize regional meetings of leaders. Global Legacy charges a fee for these services. Manwaring and other Global Legacy leaders will also travel to visit network members who invite them for advice and consultation. This "fee-for-services" model allows leaders to access revenue through the network without expecting members to donate.

Unlike HIM, Glory of Zion, and other vertical networks, Global Legacy discourages any congregation or ministry from using the name of Bethel. According to a leader in the Global Legacy network,

> You can't join us, we're not an organization...In a formal denomination, you pay for the covering, and in return you follow their rules. Our philosophy of our covering is my heart aligns with your heart. Instead of holding an umbrella over you for the covering, we give you the umbrella and you decide how you want to use it or if you want to use it at all.

Global Legacy allows Bethel to spread its vision and influence without the resources required and problems associated with creating a formal denominational organization. Because members are discouraged from using Bethel in their name, Bethel does not have to establish rules to protect its "brand" or to make sure all aligned ministries and groups adhere to their philosophy and practices. This allows Bethel simply to provide encouragement and resources to anyone who wants them.

Revenues come from the voluntary contributions of Global Legacy members, not through membership dues or any required financial commitment, as well as from members' purchasing leadership development services—leadership training courses, videoconferences, and consulting visits, for example. Global Legacy members also often purchase Bethel products such as books and other media.

Bethel is a paradigmatic example of a horizontal network because it 1) has no clear lines of authority, 2) operates primarily as a network of influence rather than governance, and 3) entails no formal ties to any particular member of the network, including formal alignment, although those in the network can claim alignment with Bethel for legitimacy.

Similar to Bethel, IHOP can be seen as a horizontal network, although the leaders of IHOP refuse to even use the word "network" because they see their connections with other organizations as even less formal than that. Instead, they describe IHOP as an "international family." There are ministries all over the world that use IHOP resources, that are led by former IHOP staff and interns, and that are influenced by IHOP beliefs and practices. Yet, as IHOP's senior leaders emphasize, "You can't join us." One such leader at IHOP explained the "nonnetwork" relationships they have with other groups and ministries:

> Up to this point there are no formal relational ties. We call it the international family of affection. We are an international family. We are nondenominational. We are not a network. We have refused to start a network for many years. At the end of this year we will host a summit. Most of the leaders from all these prayer movements are coming for the last three days of the year. That might be the closest to a networking reality that we are doing. But we're still not calling it a network. We're calling it a global conversation. We just want to talk to each other. "What are you doing? How can we help one another?" Our approach is kind of an open-source approach. What you see that is good, take it. Convert it into a product that is useful for your region. You don't have to report to us what you have done.

The main connection between IHOP and affiliated houses of prayer and ministries is personnel. An IHOP leader explained the relationship of IHOP to an affiliated group, the Pasadena International House of Prayer, or PIHOP:

> [The leader of PIHOP] comes here maybe once or twice a year. Sometimes she sees the leaders, sometimes she just spends time in the prayer room. She probably has tons of friends here. I think we operate

by friendship. There's no sending money to them or them sending money to us. One of our main guys is their main worship director. So there's a lot of exchange of personnel, because Mike [Bickle] has this open-handed policy where, "You can recruit any of my leaders without even telling me."

The goal of IHOP is to spread a practice—24/7 prayer—around the world so that Jesus will return to earth. This goal does not require the creation of a denomination or formal organization, but simply the dissemination of the idea and practice through a network of influence. According to an IHOP senior leader,

> We believe that as the day of Jesus approaches nearer and nearer, that perhaps there will be night and day prayer reality across the nations of the earth, and we want to help facilitate the conversation. In fact, there is now a conversation going whether we can divide the world into some kind of a geographical boundary and encourage the churches in every denomination around the world to take on their location and see, not having a model like this, but within one region, the whole atmosphere is covered 24/7 with prayers of the saints, so that crime will go down, evangelism will go forth. We want to facilitate that conversation.

Former IHOP Kansas City staff and interns have established houses of prayer and other groups committed to the idea of 24/7 prayer as a practice around the world. A number of these groups work with churches in their communities to hold prayer rallies, prayer walks, and 24/7 prayer vigils with the goal of "changing the atmosphere" of cities and regions to encourage them to be receptive to the message of Jesus in order to bring Jesus back to earth to begin his rule.

THE COMPETITIVE ADVANTAGE OF NETWORKS

The examples of apostolic networks that we have explored in this chapter all illustrate the advantages for religious movements of organizing in the form of a network rather than a formal organization or

denomination. We see three primary competitive advantages of networks compared with those of formal organizations in a pluralistic
religious marketplace: 1) the freedom to experiment with alternative
religious beliefs and practices without constraints imposed by a governing authority, 2) the ability of individual leaders with charisma to
expand the scale of their influence beyond their own congregations
and ministries, and 3) the ability to access revenue sources beyond
what is possible in a congregation or ministry.

THE FREEDOM TO EXPERIMENT

The most successful apostles we examined all became independent as a
result of conflicts with a formal group or denomination regarding their
unorthodox spiritual practices. John Wimber officially removed Che
Ahn from the Vineyard Association over practices resembling those of
the Toronto Blessing (an interesting development, given the fact that
Wimber was removed from Calvary Chapel about a decade earlier for
similar reasons). Similarly, Bill Johnson left the Assemblies of God
because the philosophy and practices he wanted to pursue regarding
the miraculous were incompatible with the denomination's theological
strictures.

Leaders with charisma in the Weberian sense generally do not
function well under formal bureaucracies. Boards, presbyteries, and
head offices get nervous when these charismatic leaders do things that
are outside of established practices and beliefs. Creating a network
rather than a formal organization thus allows charismatic leaders to
experiment freely with accessing spiritual power, including fighting
the demonic, relaying words heard directly from God, attempting to
heal through prayer, encouraging uncontrolled expressions of the Holy
Spirit, and pursuing social change in their communities.

Critics of these beliefs and practices can voice their dissent or simply leave the movement, but they have no power to stop charismatic
leaders from pursuing what they think God has called them to do,
as would be the case in a formal denomination. Although charismatic religious leaders have always existed independently of religious

bureaucracies, they have not always had the ability to network easily with like-minded leaders and followers around the world.

This is a considerable competitive advantage in a pluralistic religious marketplace in which seekers and believers are always looking for new ways to access the supernatural and directly experience the divine. Leaders with charisma who are free to experiment with ways of connecting to God are therefore at a significant competitive advantage vis-à-vis bureaucracies with more standardized beliefs and practices. We explore this further in Chapter 4.

EXPANDING INFLUENCE

Networks also retain some of the advantages of a formal organization, including the ability to mobilize large numbers of people and resources in ways that expand the influence of the individual leader. The organizers of Azusa Now, for example, can put on a conference that is much larger and more impressive than an individual member could manage on his or her own. Each member can draw on his or her own reputation to attract participants from across the globe and add their uniqueness to the variety of expressions of the miraculous. They can also pool staff resources to organize these conferences. Not insignificantly, each apostle expands his or her influence in the form of book, DVD, and music sales at these conferences by exposing the followers of other apostles in the alliance to their materials. All participants return to their own ministries stronger, more influential, and with greater access to funds and resources than before the conference. When a network is composed of influential leaders with charisma, each node in the network is more powerful and influential as a part of a network than they would be standing alone.

Thus, connections with other influential charismatic leaders who are willing to collaborate for a common cause and to extend influence from their own group and across geographic boundaries are a significant competitive advantage. Leaders who are bound by formal organizational ties typically collaborate almost exclusively with those in their denomination or institutional affiliation, limiting the reach of their influence. Because formal denominations and religious organizations compete for resources and followers, they are less likely to cooperate with leaders in other denominations that might steal "market share." Unaffiliated leaders, however, have much less to lose and much more to gain by collaboration, as they are not concerned with the interests of a large institution; instead, they are primarily concerned with their own ministry and following.

Expanding Funding Sources

In the examples of apostolic networks we just explored, all leaders benefited from the ability of their network to afford access to funding sources outside of their immediate congregation or ministry. The examples show a wide range of ways that networks can lead to expanded funding. For example, Bethel—a congregation of 5,000 to 6,000—receives only 19 percent of its $37 million annual budget from donations coming from the members of that congregation. The remaining $30 million or so comes from book and DVD sales, school of ministry tuition, conference fees, music sales, and tuition for online leadership development courses, most of which is purchased by people outside the congregation who want to participate in the revival based at Bethel, but who are located all over the globe (we discuss this in more detail in Chapter 5). Che Ahn's HIM receives the bulk of its income from the more than 8,000 churches and ministries in forty-two countries that the group oversees—the spiritual blessings that come from aligning with HIM flow down and the donations flow up through the vertical network. Glory of Zion receives a large part of its funding from the more than 60,000 individuals, house churches, businesses, and nonprofit ministries that belong to its web-based network, rather than from the local congregation.

In traditional denominational structures, individual congregations are funded by the donations of members who belong to that congregation. These congregations are then required to contribute funds to the denomination of which they are a part. Thus the bulk of all funds come from individuals contributing to the donation plate on Sunday morning.

In a network structure, the sources of funds are multiplied far beyond individual church member donations, and the cost of maintaining the network is much lower than the expenses that maintaining a formal denomination requires. This frees up resources to experiment with new projects and to pay high-profile individual leaders. In other words, more funding can go into activities that draw new followers, while much less is spent on staffing and running programs for local congregations.

Non-INC Examples of Network Governance

INC Christian groups are not the only example of religious leaders and ministries that are spreading their influence using a network governance structure rather than a formal denominational model. For example, the Willow Creek Association (WCA) shares many similarities with INC networks in its organizational configuration. Willow Creek Community Church, a nondenominational megachurch, was founded in 1975 in a movie theater in the suburbs of Chicago by dynamic evangelical pastor Bill Hybels. Hybels applied entrepreneurial skills in marketing evangelical Christianity to "seekers"—people unaffiliated with any church tradition who were looking for spiritual guidance and meaning in their lives. He did this by creating a comfortable, nonthreatening environment with entertaining church services, along with a myriad of programs appealing to members of the community (Hamilton 2000; Sargeant 2000). This strategy became highly successful, and the church has grown to over 23,000 attendees at Sunday services.

In 1991 Hybels formed the WCA to spread the principles by which his church became so large. The WCA now holds conferences around the world as well as workshops for pastors, which include leadership training and access to other leaders in the WCA network. Its signature event, the yearly Global Leadership Summit, is described on the WCA website as follows:

> The Global Leadership Summit is a two-day, world-class leadership event experienced by more than 170,000 leaders around the world, representing more than 14,000 churches. It's telecast live from Willow's campus every August. Throughout the fall, Summit events take place in an additional 300+ cities, 100+ countries—and translated into 50+ languages. This event is crafted to infuse vision, skill development, and inspiration for the sake of local church transformation (WCA 2015).

For $249 a year any church can become a member of the WCA as long as they affirm a commitment to "a historic, orthodox understanding of biblical Christianity." Like INC networks, the WCA does not seek to franchise congregations with the Willow Creek name, formally train or ordain pastors, or oversee churches. Much like Bethel's Global Legacy network, it simply offers products and services to anyone willing to purchase them and seeks to influence followers and congregations by teaching a specific set of principles and techniques. The WCA's network now includes nearly 9,000 congregations (Chu 2010), 53 percent of which are outside of the United States.

Another example is the Leadership Network, a Dallas-based nonprofit started by Bob Buford, a successful Harvard-educated entrepreneur and innovator in the cable TV business. He is also a protégée of management guru Peter Drucker. Buford cofounded the Leadership Network in 1984 with the goal of bringing together successful church leaders to learn from each other's leadership principles, share ideas, and create innovative strategies to lead their ministries. The network then trained other pastors and nonprofit leaders to apply those principles. Buford also founded the Peter F. Drucker Foundation for Non-Profit management, which later became the Drucker Institute at Claremont Graduate University.

Buford's leadership network brings together high-profile megachurch pastors in "leadership communities" and "innovation labs" where they share ideas and create principles for effective church leadership. The stated goal of the network is to "foster innovation movements that activate the church to greater impact." The growth of this leadership network has involved a number of well-known megachurch pastors such as Rick Warren, Bill Hybels, Tim Keller, Marc Driscoll, and Erwin McManus, as well as business icon Philip Anchutz (Stetzer 2014). The network's website claims that its weekly newsletter goes to over 60,000 leaders around the world, its books have sold over 1 million copies, and 50,000 Christian leaders around the world have participated in its global online conferences. As a whole, the network claims to serve more than 200,000 Christian leaders around the world every year. In 2012 the churches in the leadership network sold over $1 billion worth of goods and services to members of their communities.

Buford's leadership network seeks to influence pastors and leaders by promoting innovative leadership and management strategies, rather than through techniques for accessing the supernatural, like those promoted by INC leaders. Despite their differences, the Leadership Network looks similar to INC networks because it is not creating a "movement" or franchising congregations; rather, it is promoting a set of principles through conferences, events, and media products. The network's influence is hard to detect because it lacks the large organizational structure usually associated with denominational name branding. Yet the network's influence is clear in the way that churches and ministries have adopted its principles.

THEORETICAL IMPLICATIONS

We began the chapter with an explication of Max Weber's concept of charisma and the problem Weber observed in the tendency for charismatic authority to be routinized into bureaucratic–legal authority once the leader dies or can no longer manage the size of his or her religious movement. Bureaucratic–legal structures allow a movement to grow to a much larger scale than would be possible under a single leader and enable the movement to span multiple generations. This comes with a cost, however—the loss of the energy, passion, vision, and charisma of the original leader who sparked the movement in the first place. Thus, although formally organized religious movements can grow larger than a single leader's congregation and can last over numerous generations, over time they often decline in their ability to draw new adherents and may eventually begin to stagnate.

Leaders of the fastest-growing INC groups are consciously trying to opt out of the cycle of routinization of charisma through a networked form of governance that they call apostolic leadership. Under a networked structure, charismatic leaders are free to do what they do best: inspire people through their heroic acts, innovative thinking, and ability to access supernatural forces to produce the miraculous. Networks of charismatic leaders also, according to proponents, solve the problem of sustaining a large movement over time. Instead of a single charismatic leader's creating a bureaucratic–legal organization to live on beyond his or her lifetime, groups of charismatic leaders can form a decentralized network that is not dependent on any one leader. Thus when one leader dies or loses his or her following for some reason, his or her followers can simply migrate to another leader in the network—moving from one charismatic apostle to another. New apostles are constantly incorporated into the network, bringing new energy and followers of their own, so that, over time, one generation of apostles in the network is replaced by younger apostles.

In the last three decades or so, a large body of scholarship has emerged to examine the increasing use of network forms of governance, particularly within industries. "Network governance" (Jones et al. 1997), "network forms of organization" (Powell 1990), "inter-firm networks" (Uzzi 1996; 1997), and "flexible specialization" (Piore and Sabel 1984) are terms that scholars in the sociology of organizations have used to describe production systems that are organized by informal networks of cooperation rather than by bureaucratic structures within firms or legally binding contractual relationships between firms.

These theorists emphasize the competitive advantages of network governance when demand conditions are unstable—that is, when consumers' tastes for particular products change rapidly, or when consumer-spending levels are in flux (Piore and Sabel 1984). Under these conditions, networks of cooperative firms can respond to changing demands for products by coming together for short-term production runs, allowing resources to be reallocated quickly and cheaply when conditions change (Jones et al. 1997). This keeps long-term investment costs low as firms combine their resources for short-term projects. The lack of legally binding contracts also allows for flexibility and lower fixed costs (Powell 1990).

Trust must be developed between firms, however, in the absence of binding contracts. And when demand conditions are stable, it becomes more advantageous to invest in long-term contracts and equipment that allow for large production runs of standardized goods, which become cheaper per unit as the scale of production increases (Piore and Sabel 1984).

In our view there are parallels between the religious economy and the global capitalist economy in terms of demand conditions and the resulting advantages of organizing a production process around networks rather than around bureaucratic hierarchies. Networks are more flexible, reduce overhead costs, and encourage innovative responses to shifts in market demand.

We propose that INC Christianity is growing in a declining market for religious goods at least in part because of its network structure of governance.

We think that the success of INC Christianity is related to the conditions that gave rise to network forms of governance in other sectors of society.

Apostolic networks are the religious economy's version of the flexible global production networks that have transformed global capitalism. As we have seen, leaders with charisma can join together for particular projects and leverage their ability to mobilize resources and people, while at the same time retaining their autonomy to experiment and innovate with new beliefs and practices. This structure is more suited to identifying and meeting the needs of new generations of religious seekers and believers than are large-scale bureaucracies in the form of denominations, which produce highly standardized

72

religious "goods" in the form of liturgies, doctrinal statements, systematic theologies, and rituals. Like large hierarchical corporations, denominations are losing market share. If this is the case, we expect that Charismatic networks will continue to gain their "market share" of religious believers compared with standardized congregations that are part of formal denominations. This has profound implications for the way that Christianity (and other religions) are experienced and practiced, which we explore in the next chapters.

CHAPTER FOUR

THE PRODUCT

SUPERNATURAL POWER

AND SOCIAL TRANSFORMATION

In this chapter we explore the "product" that INC Christianity is promoting and why this product seems to be uniquely positioned to continue to gain "market share," particularly among young people in America's current religious marketplace. The product INC Christianity provides includes 1) direct access to miraculous power, 2) opportunities for participation in public practices, and 3) a narrative of supernatural social transformation. Although most other religious groups provide religious goods that contain one or more of these elements, INC Christianity provides all three in ways that make their product uniquely potent and compelling. To begin this discussion, we describe below the stories of people of various ages and life situations who were drawn to INC Christian activities and groups.

DARIUS MORADI

Darius, a US-born son of Persian immigrants, is in his mid-40s and works as an information technology (IT) specialist in Southern California. He became a Christian through an evangelical campus ministry in college. Since then, he has attended a number of churches and has changed congregations several times recently in an attempt to learn more about God and have opportunities to learn how to spread

God's love to others. Evangelism has always been something in which he has wanted to be involved.

Ten years ago, Darius, his wife, and their daughter left a small non-denominational evangelical church for a much larger, neo-Charismatic congregation. According to Darius, this new church emphasized evangelism but used the method of "sharing tracts" (pamphlets) containing a simple version of the gospel with people in public areas. This church is Charismatic, and according to Darius the main "gift of the spirit" that the congregation emphasizes is speaking in tongues.

In 2008, a co-worker of Darius' invited him to a "prophetic evangelism" conference. Even though Darius had attended a neo-Charismatic church for some time, he encountered things at this conference that he had not experienced before in his many years as a believer. A woman at the conference "gave him a prophetic word" in which she "read his mail," meaning that she told him things about his life that there is no way she could have known beforehand. In another session, the session leader showed a movie clip from an INC film called "The Finger of God," which highlighted ordinary people experiencing extraordinary miracles in public settings. Darius became excited about the possibility of experiencing these things himself:

> I thought, wow, that is something that would really be cool to be able to do, pray for people and see them be healed. It was intriguing to me because it wasn't being done just by a pastor or some leader in the church. It was something that I wanted to see happen in my life.

In another session at the same conference, a live web stream was shown of a revival happening in Lakeland, Florida, led by INC evangelist Todd Bentley. After the conference, Darius began watching Bentley's web streams on his computer at home. Bentley would regularly say, "If you want this anointing, you can have it by putting your hands on the computer screen and receive it," and Bentley would then pray for those wanting to receive the anointing of the Holy Spirit. Darius did this, placing his hands on the computer screen while Todd Bentley prayed. Soon afterward, a colleague at Darius's work complained of severe pain in her arm. Darius asked if he could pray for her arm. He put his hand on her arm and prayed for healing using Todd Bentley's method, saying "Fire" at the conclusion of his prayer. The colleague told Darius that his hand felt really hot. She felt heat all the way up and down her arm and the pain was relieved. This experience left Darius in tears of excitement.

Darius began walking around downtown Los Angeles on his lunch break to look for people who seemed to be in pain or struggling with a problem. When he found such a person, he would ask if he could pray for them. He brought a co-worker who speaks Spanish to translate for Spanish speakers. As a result of his prayers, he said he saw a number of people get healed from pain, sickness, and other problems.

Darius and his family decided to attend the church where the prophetic evangelism conference was held, even though it was an hour's drive from their home. This INC church is part of Bethel's "Global Legacy" network and holds classes on healing and prophecy using Bethel materials. Through his connection with this church, Darius began to participate in a ministry on Tuesday nights in which a group of fifteen to twenty people from all over Southern California gather to pray for people to be healed at the emergency room at Los Angeles County-USC Medical Center, near downtown Los Angeles—the largest public hospital in the region.

We accompanied Darius to one of these healing sessions at LA County-USC on a Tuesday night. Approximately fifteen people met at the designated time outside the door of the emergency room and prayed together before they entered. Many had driven over an hour to get there from various Southern California suburbs. Once they entered the emergency room, they spread out individually and began to approach people in the waiting area. The room was packed with hundreds of people who appeared to be mostly Latino and working class and who had been waiting for long periods of time. This emergency room is one of the few that provides care for people without insurance in the downtown LA area, and was filled with people suffering from a variety of ailments from a case of the shingles to stage 4 cancer and everything in between.

As the healers approached the emergency room patients, they would say, "I just wanted to ask you how you are doing and if you are in any pain." Most people responded by saying that yes, they were in pain, and by sharing what, in particular, was hurting. The healers would then ask, "Would you be willing to let me pray for you to take away your pain?" Roughly a quarter of the patients refused to be prayed for, but the other three-quarters agreed. If they agreed, the healers prayed for them, all of them using a similar technique. They would instruct the patient to say, "Jesus I am precious to you and I know you want to heal me"; then they would place their hand on the body part that was in pain (in "sensitive" body areas the healer would have the patient put their own hand on the body part, and the healer would place his or her hand on the patient's hand). Then they would pray something to the effect of, "God we know you love Jessica and want her to be healed, so heal her." Then they would state, "By the authority of Jesus—pain be gone."

The healer would then ask the patient whether the pain was still there. In a few cases the patient looked and acted surprised and said that the pain was gone. In most other cases, the patient said that the pain was still there but "felt better." The healer would then ask the patient "on a scale of one to ten, what is your pain level?" The patient would give a number, then the healer would say, "Okay, we are going to take it down to zero," then repeat the same prayer technique. The healer reprised this process as long as the patient was willing to continue or until the patient reported that the pain was gone.

There may have been a social incentive for some of the patients to report that their pain was gone in order to have the healer stop repeatedly trying to heal them. However, it did appear that several patients that night genuinely believed that they were healed as a result of the prayer. One man with crutches began walking around the emergency room without his crutches with an astonished look on his face, saying that he had been healed. The majority of the patients said their pain "felt better," but that they were still experiencing some pain.

After the healers had prayed for people in the emergency room for about an hour, a security guard entered the area and shouted, "All people who are not patients must leave the emergency room immediately," clearly aiming his remarks at Darius and his companions. The healers, unfazed by the order, finished their prayers and slowly walked out of the emergency room into the pharmacy waiting area and began to pray for people there. We asked one of the healers how he felt about getting kicked out of the emergency room, and he replied, "It's not a big deal; they kick us out every week." Apparently the security guards allow the healers into the room for a certain amount of time and then ask them to leave.

Most of the fifteen or so healers were from different parts of Southern California and from different churches. None were pastors or paid church workers. A significant number of them, including a man in his 30s who seemed to be the main leader of this Tuesday night healing ministry, did not attend church at all. We asked this leader why he did not attend church. He replied that there were no churches in his area that had an accurate view of God's power and desire to heal people. This man, instead, was influenced by the teachings and media presence of various INC leaders like Bill Johnson.

On the drive home, Darius and two of his friends were ecstatic over the miracles they had witnessed. They recounted stories of healings that night and on other nights with an almost manic enthusiasm and parted vowing to be at the hospital again the following Tuesday.

KAITLYN CROSBY

Kaitlyn Crosby, a student at an evangelical college on the West Coast, is in her early 20s. Although her college has roots in conservative fundamentalism, it hosts a Charismatic ministry group on campus, and Kaitlyn is one of the group's main leaders. Kaitlyn grew up in evangelical churches, but says she was not a true believer until well into her college years. Interestingly, after high school, she moved to Texas to become an intern at an INC youth organization called Teen Mania, even though she claims that at the time she was not a believer. She was drawn to the organization because it offered opportunities to travel overseas:

I like traveling [laughs]. I like the experience of going to other countries, and I knew the Gospel well enough to be able to go and be Christian but not really be Christian [laughs]. So I'd go on these mission trips, and I went to different conferences that they put on, but it was never really my own faith, it was just something that I did.

I wonder how common true is

It was through this organization that she first came in contact with "tongues and the joy of the spirit." Teen Mania has ties to the IHOP in Kansas City. Representatives from IHOP speak at Teen Mania events, and Teen Mania alum often become interns and staff members at IHOP. Kaitlyn visited IHOP while she was an intern at Teen Mania and was drawn to the passionate prayer and worship she saw there. It was through these experiences that she decided "to commit her life to Jesus" and began to see her faith as her own. After her internship ended, she enrolled in the evangelical university that she currently attends.

At this university, Kaitlyn was attracted to the Charismatic ministry group on campus because it was playing IHOP music at the outdoor ministry fair on campus:

I was like, "Oh, my gosh, that's music from IHOP!" And I recognized it, so I went over there, because I hadn't seen any of that stuff, and I had come to identify IHOP with Christians who are very passionate. That's what I was looking for when I came to [this college], I was specifically looking for people who were praying, and I didn't see a lot of really passionate stuff happening.

This campus ministry invited representatives from IHOP to campus and had them lead worship, healing sessions, and other events. The group also has connections with INC groups Youth With a Mission (YWAM) and Bethel. Kaitlyn and other leaders established a "house of prayer" on campus—which, along the lines of IHOP Kansas City's 24/7 prayer room, held continuous prayer and worship from 10 pm to 8 am every night. Kaitlyn also spent a summer at a house of prayer in Jerusalem that was modeled after IHOP, where participants conduct

24/7 prayer for the salvation and protection of Israel as well as for all of the nations of the world to become Christian.

Interestingly, the campus ministry that Kaitlyn was leading included members who were connected to both IHOP and Bethel, and those two connections shaped the group in a number of ways:

> It's funny, because IHOP and Bethel are very similar, but they're also very different. They feel very different. Bethel is very focused on joy and heaven and miracles and healings, and IHOP is very focused on prayer and intercession and worship, praying for the nations and Jesus coming back. That's what they teach, so IHOP's very heavy and Bethel's very light. They actually draw two different kinds of people to them. So you have the people who love Bethel, and then you have the people who love IHOP, and it's like, in the group, there are both kinds of people, but at first, it was more like IHOP-type people, that more heavy, pray for revival, interceding. And then kind of like over the past three years, it's transitioned more towards Bethel.

Clearly, Bethel and IHOP are the main influences in the Charismatic ministry at this historically anti-Charismatic evangelical college. When we asked Kaitlyn what the attraction is to INC groups among young people who, like her, have been raised in traditional evangelicalism, she said,

> I think energy and passion and seeing a faith that looks like it's alive. A lot of it is a reaction to the very traditional, dry kind of—I don't want to say baby boomer generation, but that kind of faith that's very, "We just want our nice Christianity and our little white picket fences." It's a reaction against that, because my generation is very justice-oriented, very action-oriented. They just want to go out and do things. So the folks at the ministries, it's always external, it's always about going out and doing stuff... So I think seeing that it's alive, seeing the miraculous, seeing people get healed, having that experience and knowing that there's more to Christianity than what

I thought, that's really attractive. I think that's what the attraction was for me—seeing that there's more to it than just what I learned growing up. There is a real God who's really alive and really wants to speak to people, and one of the ways that he speaks is through miracles and works of prophecy... I think especially twenty-somethings are looking for a purpose and an identity, and the Charismatic movement has that to offer.

Interestingly, although Kaitlyn attends church regularly, she says that many of the young people she comes in contact with through IHOP, Bethel, YWAM, and other INC groups don't attend church and are critical of traditional denominational groups:

I've come across a lot of people who are very rebellious against denominational churches and established churches, and they look at those churches and say, "They don't know what they're doing because they don't have the fire."

For many of Kaitlyn's friends, prayer and worship events, conferences, mission trips, ministry schools (like YWAM, Bethel, and IHOP), and web-based content have replaced involvement in brick-and-mortar congregations.

JOSH BRADLEY

Josh Bradley is in his early 20s and in his fourth year at IHOPU in Kansas City. He also calls himself an "intercessory missionary," a term that many staff and interns at IHOP use to describe themselves; Josh has a business card with this title under his name. He grew up in a Charismatic family in Minneapolis—he says "my parents were Jesus people back in the day"—and describes his faith in this way: "I guess you would say I was a prophetic intercessor since I was a child. I would get strong impressions and dreams. I'd have many dreams a night, and the Lord would just speak to me what he was about to do."

Josh claims that he had been receiving prophecies directly from God about Kansas City at an early age:

> When I was 10 years old, I began to pray for Kansas City. I was very close to the Holy Spirit at a young age, and when I would read books or magazines or hear about the Kansas City Chiefs, I would just begin to pray for Kansas City. I knew that God was going to do something so amazing in that city that some day when I was an adult I would end up living there. So I've been praying for Kansas City since I was 10 years old, knowing that God was going to do something significant there.

Josh heard about IHOP as a teenager in 2006 through a friend, who invited him to an IHOP-influenced prayer meeting in Minneapolis. This led him to attend IHOP's annual One Thing conference in Kansas City in 2006, a four-day event that includes top worship musicians, INC speakers from around the nation, and heavy doses of prophecy and healing from top INC leaders. This experience proved to be life changing for Josh:

> I came to Kansas City, and when I stepped into the atmosphere of God's presence, I began just to weep. I felt God's presence so heavily, and when I came to the Lord several years ago, I said, "Lord, if there's a job that exists out there where I can fast and pray and worship and sing to you, I want that job."

Several years later, Josh moved to Kansas City to enroll in IHOPU. He described his most significant experience at IHOP as a visitation by the Holy Spirit that happened in his third year as a student there:

> [I]n one of our classes in the morning, the Holy Spirit came. We'd been praying that God would send the Holy Spirit just like in the book of Acts, chapter 2, and we believe that the Lord has done that. One of the classes went from I'd say about 100 students, and by way of text messages and phone calls, by that night there was about 2,500 that had

gathered from the International House of Prayer in other areas to an auditorium to meet God. God's presence could be felt in a thick, tangible way, so heavy, as lives were completely changed. The Lord started off with inner healing, bringing his love and his kindness to people, and it's progressed into many physical healings. When I got the text message, I was really thrilled to go. I didn't know what it would look like when I got there. But when I got to the classroom I saw so many of my classmates that—they were on the floor, on their knees, some on their faces, just weeping before the presence of God. There was spontaneous singing that erupted, where different musicians and singers just went up to the stage and began to sing spontaneous songs that have never been heard before.

And then Wes Hall and some others ended up taking leadership of the meeting and began to operate in words of knowledge and words of wisdom, like Corinthians mentions the Charismatic gifts. So as the words of knowledge were being given out that people were struggling with, depressions and eating disorders and even suicide at the Bible college, all of these students began to raise their hands and admit, "Yes, I have been struggling with depression or an eating disorder." So it began as just an inner healing process of the Holy Spirit, really releasing the truth of the Father's love to the class and to the greater body gathered at IHOP.

The meetings have gone on. The praying still continues 24/7, but we've had meetings now Wednesday through Saturday from 6 to midnight, so thousands of people have come from all over the world and have been healed and refreshed. The Holy Spirit is making all the things in the Bible come true. There's a body of people that have gathered that have said yes to the things of the Holy Spirit. So he's really moved—he's really moving in such a profound way.

We baptized over 1,900 people, water-baptized, and we've seen at least over 7,000 documented healings, cancers, backs, dental miracles, teeth growing in people's mouths. I've seen legs grow out [laughs]. It's been really exciting to get to have been a part of it. We have prophecies in Kansas City particular to IHOP that no sickness and no disease known to man will stand, meaning, it doesn't matter that if anybody has AIDS or cancer, if they come to Kansas City and they have a heart that says yes to Jesus, that they want Jesus and they want to live, that the Lord will heal them.

At the time of the interview, Josh was in California with a group of 300 students from IHOPU, traveling around college campuses, holding healing and prophecy meetings and encouraging students to start houses of prayer on each college campus. Josh said that they had received prophecies that California was going to be the epicenter of another outpouring of the Holy Spirit that would lead to a revival in the United States. The trip was a preparation for this revival by sharing these prophecies with college students and encouraging them to pray for the outpouring of the Holy Spirit to come. The trip culminated in a four-day prayer conference that featured INC leaders Cindy Jacobs and Lou Engle, and that was held in a Korean American, neo-Charismatic megachurch near downtown Los Angeles.

The Selling Points of INC Christianity

Our interviews with participants of various ages and ethnicities yielded similar responses as to what drew them to these INC activities and what draws others to them. We conclude that the product sold by INC leaders has three compelling components that are driving the growth of these movements: 1) experiences of the miraculous, 2) opportunities for individuals' direct participation in these miraculous occurrences, and 3) the promise of social transformation. It is not that these three components are unique to INC Christianity. Most Christian groups, particularly Pentecostal groups, offer one or more of these three elements. However, INC Christianity has packaged these components in ways that many people, particularly young adults, find extremely attractive.

Experiences of the Miraculous

These three participants, as well as the others we interviewed, were all drawn to INC activities primarily to experience the miraculous.

Recall Darius's statement: "That is something that would really be cool to be able to do, pray for people and see them be healed." According to Darius, that is something he now experiences weekly at the LA County-USC Hospital emergency room and on his peripatetic healing lunch breaks at work. Kaitlyn stated that the main draw of these groups for young people is "seeing that it's alive, seeing the miraculous, seeing people get healed, having that experience." Josh was drawn to IHOP though his experiences of dreams and visions as well as his participation in the One Thing conference, where he felt God's presence so "heavily" that "he began to weep." Others reported experiences with demonic spirits and visionary dreams which they needed help interpreting and responding to. Still others reported being approached by someone who gave them a "prophetic word from the Lord" or "read their mail"—revealing information that the person could not have known had they not been given a special revelation from God.

One of the participants of Bethel's School of Supernatural Ministry explained the attraction of Bethel for young people in this way:

> Our culture is so focused on experience. The idea of a God who interacts with us in a physical and tangible way—it's not new, but it hasn't been the emphasis in whole congregations. Bethel—I feel like it's the first church that is actually preaching: "God touches you and wants to touch you." That draws in people who do really want an experience with God. Whether that's a healing or understanding his love, or need a destiny or a purpose in life, or financial breakthrough. On the one hand I think it attracts really needy people, but on the other hand it really attracts people who really do want to change the world and [who] want to understand the power of God. So I think it attracts two different polar opposites of kinds of people. People who are so desperate for a father and something to just touch them and change everything and then people who are like oh yeah, I'm going to change the world.

One high-profile INC leader we interviewed, whose ministry has a large young adult contingent, used similar terms to explain his perspective:

Well, we're drawing in a lot of young people. What's drawing them is, first of all, we're not religious. They want authenticity, they want real power, and when we pray for the sick, the way we worship, it's like, they want to encounter God, not just learn about God intellectually. They're engaged in that. Praying for the signs and wonders. They see the super-natural, they're very interested in the supernatural. Even the dark side of it is huge with the "Twilight" series. People are looking for reality, and the advantage of being Charismatic is that we have a theology for this, so we can practice it. We're seeing a wave of young people being attracted to our church because of that supernatural Charismatic culture that I think is more conducive for this generation than a traditional church setting where they just—maybe a good message, nice songs, but it doesn't hit them, *it's the experience.*

In sum, the promise of direct experience with supernatural forces appears to be particularly attractive to young people.

At Bethel School of Supernatural Ministry the philosophy of teaching, as expressed by one of its senior leaders, is, "How do we get our students to experience what we're teaching?" This leader describes a typical day in the life of the ministry school:

So I would be like, "Okay, today I'm going to teach on deliverance [from demonic spirits]. The students don't know that." We're, like, two months into school. We did worship, and then they were doing some testimonies, and I walk in halfway through the testimonies, and this third person is sharing a testimony; instead of sharing a testimony, she says, "There's this thing inside me that is telling me what to do, and I have no control over it. I think it's a demon." And of course, she's weeping. "And this thing has me and it makes me do evil things." And she's going through this thing and she's weeping, and I'm sitting in the back at the table, and I had this sudden thought, like, "I'm teaching on deliverance, and she's telling me she needs a deliverance." So from the back of the room, I shout, "Jesus is going to deliver you right now." And when I said that, she falls to the ground and she starts crawling around like a snake. This is one of my students. And our other students

86

are like—they had never seen anything like that. I've done hundreds of deliverances, so I'm like, "Well, that was pretty wild." So I tell our students, I said, "Get around, I'm going to show you how to do a deliverance." So instead of using my notes, I'm like, I just walk 'em through.

While we started delivering this one girl, two more of my students manifest [channeling demonic spirits]. They fall down on the ground and they start screaming and things start screaming out of them. These are my students. I have three students who are literally demonized. And so while we're trying to get this one girl delivered, two more students manifest. They're on the floor floppin' around, screaming, doing crazy stuff, and I'm like, "OK, so let's stop for a minute. Let's break into three groups. You guys go there. You 10 go there, you 10 here, you 10 over there. You take the lead, you take the lead there, you take the lead there. I'll tell you what to do. This is what we're going to do."

This "extreme" type of experiential learning in the realm of the supernatural is precisely what attracts many students to BSSM.

Prophecy, healing, and delivering people from evil spirits are obviously not new to Pentecostalism. Along with speaking in tongues (which is notably absent from most INC activities), these manifestations of the Holy Spirit have been the hallmarks of Pentecostal/Charismatic practice throughout its history. INC groups, however, place these activities at the center of their ministries. Then they take them out of the context of church and into the public realm, where they are able to experiment with them to a much greater extent than other Pentecostal groups.

For example, one of the activities for students at BSSM is a Thursday night "treasure hunt." Every Thursday a large group of students breaks up into groups of three or four to pray for a vision from God for where they should go and what they should do that night. They then receive words or images from God that direct what they should do next. Someone might get a vision of "ice cream" or a "blue sign" or something of that nature. The groups then discuss what the vision or word might mean, then they act on it. Perhaps they will drive around looking for an ice cream shop with a blue sign. Once they find what they're looking for, they then pray that God will give them a vision for what to do next.

Often they will sense that God wants them to talk to a particular person in the place that He has led them to, which often prompts the team to pray for the person's healing or deliverance from some form of suffering. These teams return to the school enthusiastically relaying accounts of God's miraculous intervention. We spoke to a waitress in the town of Redding, California, where BSSM is located, and she commented that on Thursday nights the residents brace for the influx of Bethel students coming to talk and pray with people, which is not always appreciated.

Another group that identified itself with Bethel set up a "prophecy booth" in a neighborhood farmers market in a Southern California suburb. They created a square space on the pavement with duct tape and a sign advertising prophecy and words from the Lord to anyone interested.

The person who was praying for a "word from the Lord" told a "customer" that he envisioned him in a corner office of a high building somewhere—suggesting that God will place him in an influential position in the business world where he will shape the world for God. The recipient of the prophecy, a high school teacher, was more than a little skeptical of the prophecy.

These types of public activities are highly experimental and sometimes subject to criticism and even scorn in the communities in which they operate. But they also offer possibilities of thrilling supernatural experiences for participants. Because of the loose organizational structure of these groups, experimentation is not only allowed but also encouraged. Because there is very little oversight over the use of particular techniques or theological discussion of the appropriateness of various techniques or practices, INC individuals and groups can develop practices that are public, participatory, and previously untested. More established Pentecostal groups try to limit the extent to which their members engage in potentially controversial or invasive practices by keeping rituals that access the supernatural in a more controlled environment.

OPPORTUNITIES FOR PARTICIPATION AND LEADERSHIP

According to many of our respondents, people are drawn to INC groups because of the opportunities to directly participate in miraculous phenomena, generate their own ideas, and lead their own ministries. Recall Darius's statement that the possibility of healing people in public "was intriguing to me because it wasn't being done by a pastor or some leader in the church. It was something that I wanted to see happen in my life." He was excited because anyone, including him, could participate in the supernatural. Recall Kaitlyn's statement that "my generation is very justice-oriented, very action-oriented. They just want to go out and do stuff." She saw IHOP and Bethel as groups in which young people could take action and participate, rather than simply listen and watch "official" leaders do the work.

According to the leader of a large YWAM base in Southern California, young people are drawn to opportunities to come up with their own ideas and lead without much training or experience:

> A lot of our young people are very idealistic; they're almost activistic. They want to do something. They don't want to just hear about it, they want to actually make a difference. They come to YWAM and they want to see something change . . . they don't want to just hear about it. They want to go out and meet a sinner, somebody who's got problems and help alleviate their problem. They're very hands-on, activistic kind of people, for sure.
>
> [Here] they can make a contribution, whereas in a lot of churches, unfortunately, it's more like, "That's what *they* do. They get to do all the decision-making, all the leading. We're just little pawns." There's a lack of vision and enthusiasm.

This leader also talked about the skepticism that youth have for organizational leadership and their desire to take on and start their own ministries:

> Really, titles don't mean anything to these guys. They are very well empowered with their little computers and all their stuff in terms of

information. What they want to see is relationship. They want to see the body of Christ functioning the way it's supposed to, or the way they think it's supposed to, and I think it gives them hope to see that the gap, the power gap, I guess you'd call it, is not as large any more. We don't require them to jump through a lot of hoops in terms of the training before they get to go somewhere. We let them dream and explore and hear from God, and we think we trust young people, we really do. There's just a fundamental trust. And often they fail us, and often they make mistakes. But we're still like, "Hey, you guys can do it. You can do something for the Lord. You can make a difference for God at 18 or 20 or 22. You don't have to wait until you're experienced, 30 and dead" [laughs]. It's really, they know when they come to YWAM, they get to do stuff.

This desire, particularly among young people, to "go out and do stuff" rather than simply listen to preaching or watch others lead worship or perform miracles is a primary attraction to experimental and loosely structured INC groups. We heard this repeatedly from participants and leaders alike. A senior leader from IHOP cited the desire for a challenging, fervent environment with leadership opportunities for young people as central to why they are drawing so many young people:

[The attraction] would be number one, the fervency. Young people need something to live for and something to die for. Mediocre reality does not attract them. Mike [Bickle]'s teaching, it is very challenging. It connects the young person to an eternal cause. So young people, because of fervency, the message, and then the young leadership that is leading this movement want to be here. Young people are attracted to young people leading the movement. They say, "I can do that. If he can do that, I can do that." So you have the 18-year-old looking at a 22-year-old. "Wow, you're really, really mature." And Mike [Bickle] would release them to preach at conferences, and you have senior pastors coming from Korea, looking forward to some famous speaker, and they look at this kid speaking and say, "He's younger than my son!"

The lack of formal leadership structures in INC groups, and the fact that they are not organized primarily around congregations or Sunday services, opens possibilities for more participation than would be the case in a traditionally organized denominational religious group.

SOCIAL TRANSFORMATION

Another attraction, particularly among young people, of INC groups seems to be the promise of not simply seeing individuals get healed or "saved," but rather being a part of bringing in wholesale social transformation. The desire of young evangelicals to participate in "social justice" activism has been noted by a number of commentators and scholars (see, for example, Carpenter 2003; Gerson 2006; Bernstein 2007). Justice, however, seems to be loosely defined in evangelical circles and mostly refers to charity and social service activities rather than political advocacy. Still, many INC groups have ideas about social transformation that break from traditional evangelical interest in "helping" and "social service" ministries. They see the current time in history as one in which God is bringing "heaven to earth" through appointed "apostles" who will transform entire cities, governments, cultures, and nations. According to a leader in the New Apostolic Reformation,

> The goal of this new movement is transforming social units like cities, ethnic groups, nations rather than individuals. This has really taken off in the last 10 years or so among independent Charismatic groups that are not affiliated with a particular denomination.
>
> So the idea behind it theologically is that they believe that they need to retake the dominion that Satan stole from Adam in the Garden of Eden. Now, since Jesus came, now they believe that they can retake that dominion and advance the kingdom of God socially, not just making individual converts. They are advancing the idea of what they call the "seven mountains mandate." The seven mountains are seven sectors of society—family, government, arts and entertainment, media, business, education, and religion, and Christians are supposed to permeate

each mountain and rise to the top of each mountain. They believe if Christians permeate each mountain and rise to the top of all seven mountains, then society will be completely transformed. Society would have biblical morality, people would live in harmony, there would be peace and not war, there would be no poverty. It's really almost a utopian vision.

This idea that "kingdom-oriented" and "spirit-filled" believers will take top leadership positions in the "seven mountains"—sectors of society—to effect social transformation is a departure from classical Pentecostal theology.

This is how one high-profile INC leader described the new focus:

So our vision is not just to win souls—that is a high priority—but to disciple nations, to bring heaven's culture here on earth, to bring heaven down to earth. We've been praying that for 2,000 years, praying, "Thy kingdom come, thy will be done on earth as it is in heaven." So I think we're not just about planting churches, but we want to do what we can to eradicate systemic poverty, working with children at risk, we've rescued child soldiers and bring them into homes, do our part to stop the human trafficking in Calcutta, so there's a whole transformational element to what we're doing and our vision.

Classical Pentecostal theology tends to be premillennial, meaning that there is little hope for social improvement in the collective human condition until the millennium, when Jesus returns to rule the world. Thus the focus of the church should not be on social improvement but on saving individual souls and preparing them for the next life. The theology of many (though not all) INC groups tends to be postmillennial—meaning that God has empowered believers through the Holy Spirit to literally create heaven on earth through their gaining power in the various sectors of society. This "dominionist" theology has caused alarm among many secular observers of new INC groups.

Not surprisingly, the techniques that INC groups are promoting to facilitate this social transformation are wholly supernatural. Their methods do not involve building institutions as a power base to influence the political process, educational institutions, the media, or other powerful sectors of society. Nor do they necessarily have a specific vision as to what these sectors would look like under the control of "kingdom-minded" believers. Rather, INC groups that emphasize social transformation see their project as a "spiritual battle" that takes place in the unseen realm, where Satan and his forces control the institutions of society, and spirit-empowered believers are able to defeat those demonic forces and move into positions of authority, bringing in the reign of God on earth. Thus spiritual, not institutional, reform is what is needed in the seven mountains of society.

One set of techniques developed by leaders in the "Spiritual Warfare Network" (mentioned in Chapter 2) to transform the seven mountains for the kingdom of God is called "strategic-level spiritual warfare." These leaders have developed a protocol for defeating demonic "territorial spirits" that control certain geographic areas and thus keep Satan in charge of the seven mountains of culture in those areas. The protocol involves three strategic elements: research, prophecy, and intercession.

RESEARCH

First, the spiritual warrior must research the religious history of the area, to produce a report called a "spiritual profile." The aggregate of this research pinpoints geographic locations that are of "spiritual significance"—called spiritual "hot points" in a city or larger area. Actual maps are created, and lines are drawn between these hot points. These lines are seen as demonic corridors of power—demons travel back and forth along the transit routes. The connecting lines are seen as a "demonic stronghold."

PROPHECY

After the research stage is completed, people who are gifted in receiving direct prophecies from God are employed to determine the name

93

and nature of the demonic forces in a given area as well as the obstacles those forces have created to oppose revival and social transformation.

INTERCESSION

After the name and nature of the demonic spirits are determined through prophecy, prayer leaders called intercessors lead prayer walks, meetings, and vigils to fight the demonic spirits, calling them out by name and thereby breaking their hold on the area.

After these stages are completed, the groups organize churches and other religious leaders in a city or region to hold evangelistic campaigns and healing services, often employing civic leaders to spearhead and/or endorse the campaigns. According to the organizers of these campaigns, they have been highly successful in not only gaining converts, but also in transforming the social climate of entire cities and regions. They cite dropping rates of crime and poverty as well as the decline of other social ills.

INC leader George Otis produced a series of documentary films called "Transformations" that show how these techniques were used to allegedly bring rapid social change to several cities and regions in Africa, Latin America, and the United States.

One example of applying strategic-level spiritual warfare to produce social transformation that is highlighted in the "Transformations" series is the city of Hemet, California. Hemet is a small town in the "Inland Empire," approximately 60 miles east of Los Angeles.

Hemet-based INC leader Bob Beckett and other leaders desired to see transformation in Hemet, which had high levels of poverty and a reputation as a production site for methamphetamines. In conducting initial research on the spiritual history of Hemet, they found a number of things that they saw as relevant to the "spiritual atmosphere" of the city. First, they discovered that a church is currently located at the site of a massacre of Native Americans. Second, they found that, a number of years ago, a water company made a mistake that accidently drained the valley's underground water supply, which led to the economic decline of the area. Third, they learned that there were other religious and spiritualist movements located in the city that the INC leaders considered occult groups. Finally, they uncovered evidence that there was a history of conflict between Methodists and Pentecostals in the town. The leaders concluded that these aspects of Hemet's history were "hot spots" of demonic control.

As a result, the leaders held a spiritual warfare rally in Hemet during which white INC believers confessed to and repented for the massacre of Native Americans, a representative of the water company confessed to and repented for their mistake years ago, and participants drove stakes into the ground at the four main routes into the city and one in the city center, creating a symbolic prayer canopy over the city. They then staged a prayer vigil, calling out the demonic forces in the city. The "Transformations" video claims that, since that time, the city has been transformed, churches are growing, and crime, violence, and "occult activity" have diminished.

Another INC strategy for "taking dominion" over cities and nations is to infiltrate the seven mountains by influencing the major players in the highest levels of these sectors and by placing kingdom-minded believers in those positions. HROCK in Pasadena, for example, sees itself as uniquely positioned to influence the media and entertainment mountain because of its proximity to Hollywood. They have several strategies for doing this. First, they use their meeting facility, the Ambassador Auditorium, for various arts, media, and entertainment events. The Pasadena Symphony Orchestra now holds all of their concerts at the Ambassador. Major film and TV studios—including NBC, MTV, and Dream Works—have also rented the facility for the filming of performances. This has expanded the connections that the leadership of HROCK has with entertainers and producers in Hollywood. A prominent leader of HROCK described a more intentional strategy that they have deployed to influence the types of movies that are made in Hollywood:

> We're very conscious about what's going on in the whole [entertainment] world, because we're here in LA, and we have a lot of people working in the industry. So how can we shift things in Hollywood?

What can we do to influence the six major studios in Hollywood? So there are people who are—I had a meeting right before you came with a group of leaders who are part of this group called Genesis One Media. Their whole goal is to get the producers of these movies to guarantee the first showing of their movies in churches across America, because there are 6,000 theaters in the US but there are 400,000 churches, and if they can get, let's say, the top 100,000 involved, that's still more than 6,000 theaters. So if we could unite them, all of a sudden they're starting to make movies that are more targeted towards the church people.

Now, Mel Gibson did that with *Passion of the Christ*. He was brilliant to do that. He was just viral, his movie became a billion-dollar movie, when you include the DVD sales and all that. Same thing with *Chronicles of Narnia*. So if we can just have that system down that we could just say to these producers, "You have this natural marketing thing. We want you to reward the churches, let them have the first showing." I'm talking about quality movies, not just some church-made movies. Even *Fireproof* was good, but I'm talking about the quality like *Blind Side* or *The Passion of the Christ*. So if they could see it, it would start influencing Hollywood to say, "You know what? This is an incredible"—you know, motivated by money—"Let's start producing these movies that these church viewers want to see and get the word out to the theaters so we have already the momentum of having a blockbuster hit?"

Other groups use other techniques. IHOP, for example, has a more premillennial view of social transformation—that it is not possible to significantly improve the world until Jesus comes back to earth to begin his reign. However, they believe that they can hasten the return of Jesus to earth by setting up 24/7 houses of prayer in strategic locations. Although not officially overseeing any houses of prayer in other locations, IHOP has inspired many people to found 24/7 houses of prayer all over the world that they see as key locations in the project of bringing Jesus back soon.

The house of prayer in Jerusalem, for example, called Succat Hallel, (meaning "Tabernacle of Praise") contains an open prayer room with large·windows looking out over the old city. Prayer sessions operating 24/7 focus on praying for the salvation of the Jews, for protection over the city and nation, and for the End Times prophecies in the Bible regarding Israel to be fulfilled (premillennial theology sees Israel as the center of Jesus' coming 1,000-year reign on earth).

An IHOP-influenced house of prayer called Radiance International (RI) also exists on Sunset Blvd in Hollywood. According to one of the leaders of RI, "The Lord very clearly spoke to us about moving into the heart of the city to establish 24/7 prayer to affect culture." Their goal is not only to pray for the transformation of Hollywood, which they see as the epicenter of popular culture, but also to infiltrate the entertainment industry by making art themselves. They currently house an art gallery and have plans to start a recording studio and dance academy. Their goal is to become producers of culture that surpasses the offerings coming from "the world." One of the leaders of RI explained:

> There's a lot of people from the House of Prayer who are in the world, doing music. They are partnering with producers and stuff like that. But we feel like in the long term, where God's bringing this House of Prayer, is that we're going to be establishing our own label. We already have our own art gallery. It's going to be separate from the influence of the world in terms of, "Hey, you can do this, you can't do this," but it's going to be excellent. I believe it's going to surpass what the world has. That's going be our testimony. That's what's going to draw people to Jesus.

These leaders of RI predict that as kingdom-minded artists begin to make the best music, dance, and art, then the entire culture will be transformed. They see themselves as the epicenter of this transformation:

> We believe as God raises up real people of influence who are consecrated, that's where transformation will begin. We're believing, and that's what we're praying for, that God's going to raise up a company of people who are going to rise into great influence and are going to have a

real strong voice, and they're going to be Kingdom and they're going to be consecrated. When they speak, when they make their music, they're going to begin to really touch culture in a very broad way. I believe a transformed Hollywood begins with this company of people who belong to the Lord—their hearts belong to the Lord. As they create and make one movie, like a "Passion of the Christ" movie, or sing one song, or do a clip, whatever it is, dance a dance, that it'll captivate a generation. And if we have 10 people and then 100 people and then 1,000 people who are doing this, I think we'll begin to see a culture shift.

This model of social transformation is clearly a top-down or "trickle-down" model. As kingdom-minded believers rise to the top of the entertainment industry, the music, films, and other artworks they create will lead to the entire nation's being transformed.

Another one of the mountains targeted by INC groups is the sector of government. It is this aspect of INC "social transformation" that has received the most attention and criticism in the news media. Interestingly, again, the tactics for influencing government are almost wholly supernatural. Instead of creating a policy agenda and mobilizing resources and people to promote that platform, INC leaders instead host prayer rallies that are connected to influential conservative politicians and support individual kingdom-minded politicians in their quest for office through prayer networks and words of prophecy.

As mentioned earlier, in 2011 more than 30,000 people attended the event hosted by Rick Perry at Reliant Stadium in Houston called "The Response: A Call to Prayer for a Nation in Crisis." This event was organized by conservative evangelical political activist David Lane and funded by the American Family Association, but also included INC leaders such as Lou Engle (affiliated with both HIM and IHOP); Alice Patterson, founder of INC political group Justice at the Gate; apostle Doug Stringer, head of the INC group "Somebody Cares International;" and four senior leaders from IHOP. Texas Governor Rick Perry, an evangelical Methodist, initiated the event and was the keynote speaker. The event was highly publicized in the news media and served as a launching pad for Perry's 2012 presidential campaign.

At the event, Perry quoted from the Bible and preached about the salvation that comes from Christ, then concluded with a prayer for a country that he described as overwhelmed by problems: "We see discord at home. We see fear in the marketplace. We see anger in the halls of government." Louisiana Governor Bobby Jindal initiated a similar rally, organized by the same leaders, at the basketball arena at Louisiana State University in January of 2015. As with the Texas event, the rally at LSU was widely seen as the starting point for Jindal's run for the Republican presidential nomination in 2016.

Jindal's event had the same name as Perry's—"The Response: A Call to Prayer for a Nation in Crisis"—and even used some of the same promotional materials. The event took place on the same day as a "Right to Life" march on the campus of LSU, where Jindal also appeared as the keynote speaker.

These two events highlight the political strategies of INC leaders. Despite their linkages with prominent players in the Republican Party, the content of these events was not overtly political—they were rallies to pray and fast for God to forgive and bless the nation. But both were initiated by and highlighted prominent Christian national figures who are strong opponents of abortion and same-sex marriage—central policy priorities for conservative Christians of all stripes.

The primary INC strategies to infiltrate the government mountain are thus twofold: 1) to fast and pray for God to overcome demonic forces and to establish his reign over the nation and 2) to promote kingdom-minded individuals to the highest positions in government. Although Perry and Jindal are not Charismatics, nor do they attend INC churches or ministries, they are seen as kingdom-minded believers who would use their positions of authority to help bring in the culture and values of the kingdom through politics.

Sarah Palin is another INC kingdom-minded favorite. A Pentecostal herself—attending an Assemblies of God church in Wasilla, Alaska—Palin has ties to numerous INC leaders. While she was governor of Alaska, Palin famously was prayed over by Kenyan apostle Thomas Muthee to protect her from the "spirit of witchcraft." Conservative Republicans Newt Gingrich, Mike Huckabee, and Sam Brownback have also been linked to INC-sponsored events and leaders (Geivett and Pivec 2014).

Mike Bickle of IHOP, for example, recently endorsed Ted Cruz in his bid for the 2016 Republican nomination, sparking criticism because of Bickle's statements on gay marriage and other controversies (Johnson 2016). On his website, Cruz embraced Bickle's endorsement: "Through prayer, the Lord has changed my life and altered my family's story...I am grateful for Mike's dedication to call a generation of young people to prayer and spiritual commitment. Heidi and I are grateful to have his prayers and support" (cited in Johnson 2016).

INC prophet Lance Wallnau met with Donald Trump and endorsed his bid for the presidency, stating that, "He needs to continue his work as a wrecking ball to the spirit of political correctness that has been like witchcraft muzzling and intimidating the Christian community" (Ong 2015). In a video on his Facebook page, Wallnau prophesied, "God has given this man [Trump] an anointing for the mantle of government in the United States, and he will prosper" (cited in Ong 2015). Wallnau likens Trump to King Cyrus in the book of Isaiah, Chapter 45, which states, "This is what the Lord says to His anointed, Cyrus, whose right hand I have grasped to subdue nations before him, as I strip kings of their armor, to open doors before him and gates that cannot keep closed." Wallnau sees significance in the fact that Trump would be the forty-fifth president of the United States, which aligns with the forty-fifth chapter of Isaiah (Ong 2015).

These INC strategies differ greatly from those of other conservative evangelical groups seeking to influence policy and the political system. Groups such as the Family Research Council, the Traditional Values Coalition, the National Organization for Marriage, and other conservative groups are more traditional in their methods of mobilizing voters, setting policy goals, and lobbying candidates. Although the INC strategy of mobilizing people for prayer and supporting a few specific candidates does not seem on the surface very likely to have a great impact on the national political system, it nonetheless gives INC participants a sense that they are involved in a cosmic struggle for the redemption of the world. This sense that they are not only "saving souls" but transforming the world and defeating demonic forces is highly attractive to young believers, as they see their activities as having cosmic rather than simply local significance.

CONCLUSION: WHAT IS THE ATTRACTION?

The primary attraction to INC Christianity is clearly its experimentation with the supernatural, as it has always been the with all Pentecostal/Charismatic expressions of the Christian faith. However, it is the particular way in which INC Christianity interacts with the supernatural that has led to its emergence as the fastest-growing movement in contemporary Christianity.

Because INC Christianity is a network of independent leaders with no official overseer or denominational body, INC leaders and participants are free to experiment with innovative approaches to harnessing the supernatural. Gathering a dozen or so people in a large public emergency room to perform healing sessions on a Tuesday night would probably generate complaints from the hospital and other entities if the people came from a single congregation or traditional denomination—letters could be sent, charges could be filed, reputations would be at stake. Also, church elders or those formally trained in theology might critique the healing group's claim that "God heals everyone who asks" and could possibly forbid the group from holding these healing sessions. But if the individuals involved are not part of any one church or group, but rather part of a loose network of "free agents" inspired by live-streamed revival meetings and DVDs sold over the Internet, it becomes difficult for anyone to oppose such a gathering, other than having security guards kick participants out of the ER when they show up. The lack of formal structure in INC groups allows for undertakings that would be squelched in a traditional congregation or denomination.

Likewise, when a "larger-than-life" charismatic personality or apostle like Mike Bickle, Bill Johnson, Todd Bentley, or Che Ahn decides to implement unorthodox methods of accessing the supernatural through visions, prophecies, or exorcisms, there are no oversight bodies to tell them to tone it down or that their theology is wrong. The legitimacy of their actions derives solely from "charismatic authority" in the Weberian sense.

This lack of formal structure among INC groups also allows for more freedom for lay people to participate and lead than in a traditional congregation. We heard repeatedly from the young participants we interviewed that they were drawn to these groups because they had grown weary of simply sitting in pews, listening to orthodox teaching, watching other people lead, and having their religious activities confined to a church building. They wanted to go out and "do stuff"—heal people, cast out demons, transform cities and nations— rather than sit in church and listen to a sermon and a few songs and go home.

A number of authors have claimed that advances in digital communications technology have "flattened" organizational structures and opened new possibilities for the sharing of information, power, and leadership. In a provocative *Harvard Business Review* article, Heimans and Timms (2014) argue that technology has created a "new power" that is less hierarchical and more participatory than "old power":

New power operates differently, like a current. It is made by many. It is open, participatory, and peer driven. It uploads and it distributes. Like water or electricity, it's most forceful when it surges....New power gains its force from people's growing capacity—and desire—to go far beyond passive consumption of ideas and goods.

Heimans and Timms go on to argue that as this new power becomes more visible and integrated into peoples' lives, it produces a change in values:

Among those heavily engaged with new power—particularly people under 30 (more than half the world's population)—a common assumption is emerging: *We all have an inalienable right to participate*. [Italics added]. For earlier generations, participation might have meant only the right to vote in elections every few years or maybe to join a union or religious community. Today, people increasingly expect to actively shape or create many aspects of their lives.

Young people, according to this article, are no longer content to look to older experts and established leaders to define what is true or what is possible. They are no longer willing to passively consume the ideas and practices that leaders pass down to them. They expect to be involved in shaping their world to a greater extent than previous generations.

This parallels finding in other research on the so-called "post-boomer" generations that have come of age after the post–World War II baby boomers. Flory and Miller (2008) summarize the formative and shared experiences of individuals born in America post-1960s. First, as children of the baby boom generation, they have learned from their parents to question authority and institutions. This leads to an inclination to pursue one's own personal journey without commitment to institutional affiliations, a trend that was well articulated in Bellah et al.'s (1985) *Habits of the Heart*. The constant drumbeat of highly publicized scandals involving politicians, corporations, and religious leaders in what has become a 24/7 media-saturated environment has further intensified postboomers' suspicion of institutions.

Second, globalization has brought these generations into contact with multiple worldviews and cultures, making them more open and tolerant of different ways of understanding the world. Third, the digital revolution has democratized access to information and has made access to that information active rather than passive. Thus technology not only allows for the instant consumption of information but also allows the individual to create and shape the content that is being distributed, making the process of knowledge creation more democratic and participatory (see, for example, Burnett 2005; Hansen 2004; Ryan 2003; Tapscott 1998).

Flory and Miller (2008) go on to assert that postboomers seek an "embodied spirituality" that includes a physical experience of the sacred that is directed outward toward the communities in which they are located. They link this idea to Florida's (2002) concept of "experiential consuming" in which individuals pursue experiences not as spectators but as active participants and shapers of the experience. Flory and Miller conclude that a new form of spirituality is emerging among postboomers that they call "expressive communalism," which combines physical experiences of the sacred with an other/community orientation.

By extension (this helps to explain the attraction of INC Christianity for young adults.) It is highly experiential, participatory, and outward oriented. It operates largely outside of formal institutions, allows participation among "nonprofessional" lay people, and encourages experimentation with intense direct experiences of the supernatural. All of these factors give INC Christianity some distinctive advantages over traditional groups that are more carefully planned, limited to church settings, and led by officially trained professionals.

CHAPTER FIVE

INNOVATIONS
IN FINANCE
AND MARKETING

We have seen in the last two chapters how the organizational structure and "product" of INC Christianity is related to its success as the
fastest-growing segment of American Christianity. We now turn to
finances and marketing: How do INC groups and leaders make their
product known to the public? How do they finance their operations?
We show that the unique structure of INC Christianity, coupled with
the availability of new digital communication technologies, has created opportunities for effective marketing and alternative sources of
finance. Two cases—Bethel and IHOP—are useful in illustrating how
finance and marketing among INC groups are different from those of
traditional religious groups.

Bethel

As mentioned earlier, Bethel consists of a 6,000-member megachurch,
a School of Supernatural Ministry with 1,900 students (35 percent of
whom are international), the web-based "Global Legacy" network,
and income from conferences where Bill Johnson and other members
of the Bethel team are speaking, leading worship, or participating.
Johnson travels much of the year speaking at conferences, including
those convened by the "Revival Alliance," consisting of Johnson, Che
Ahn, John Arnott, Heidi Baker, Georgian Banov, and Randy Clark.

In our visit to Bethel in 2013, one of the leaders we interviewed broke down their roughly $37 million annual budget as given in Table 5.1.

This table contains several interesting revelations. First, only 19 percent of Bethel's revenue comes from "plate donations," also known as "tithes and offerings" from the congregation on Sunday. Thus 81 percent of Bethel's budget comes from revenue sources that are not usual for a traditionally organized religious congregation or denomination. Typically, the bulk of the income for congregations and denominations comes from donations during Sunday morning services. One study found that, on average, 91 percent of all revenue in American congregations comes from individual "plate" donations from within the congregation (US Congregational Life Survey 2008). Second, the largest income category, making up 23 percent of the total budget, is sales from media, including music CDs, DVDs, books (the Bethel staff includes more than thirty authors), and live-streamed web-based content.

Traditionally organized megachurches may use music programming, conferences, education classes, and perhaps even books written by the pastor to recruit and retain people in the congregation. In traditional

Table 5.1 Sources of Income: Bethel Redding

Income Source	Income ($ Millions)	Percentage of Budget
Plate Donations From Congregation	7	19
Web-Based Media Sales (Music, DVD's, Books, Web Content)	8.4	23
BSSM Tuition	7	19
Conferences	4	11
Global Legacy	1	3
Mission Support	1.4	4
Advance Redding	3	9
Other	5	12

Source: Interview with Bethel Leader.

congregations, however, these activities are used as "marketing" to increase membership or perhaps to supplement the income of the pastor, worship leaders, or other staff. Some leaders of these large congregations want to spread their influence beyond their congregation. Megachurch pastor Rick Warren serves as a good example. He has written several best-selling books, has a large national influence, and is involved in numerous causes internationally. But his congregation, Saddleback Valley Community Church, remains the primary focus of his ministry.

For Bethel, in contrast, the congregation, although large, is not the primary focus of the leadership. The group is not primarily concerned with building and replicating congregations, but rather with promoting techniques and practices that anyone can participate in regardless of whether they are part of a congregation. Thus, the Bethel School of Supernatural Ministry (BSSM), conferences, media sales, and web-based materials are more important to the finances of the organization than the congregation. The advantages of this, from a marketing and finance perspective, is that leadership techniques can be taught through media with very low overhead costs, and revenue can be accessed by members of the network who are far from the local congregation.

Another interesting source of funding for Bethel is Advance Redding, a separate for-profit corporation. The 2,000-seat Civic Auditorium in Redding was owned by the city and losing money. Bethel bought the auditorium and rents it out more than 120 nights a year for concerts, conferences, and other events. Advance Redding was created as a for-profit business to operate the venue—in fact, Advance Redding also rents space in the auditorium to Bethel itself as a site for its school of supernatural ministry.

We attended a conference in 2011 that was held at HROCK's Ambassador Auditorium. The conference, called "Heaven on Earth: Cultivating a Supernatural Culture," was organized by the "Revival Alliance" and featured Bill Johnson, Heidi Baker, John Arnott, Che Ahn, Georgian Banov, and Randy Clark as the headline speakers.

Each speaker taught from the Bible for an hour or so, but the main events seemed to be either before or after the Bible teaching session, when the leader would bring people on stage to be prayed over for healing. Many on stage confessed to being healed of injuries, chronic pain, and other ailments. During these healing sessions, the excitement in the room built to a crescendo, and some were falling down and "laughing in the spirit." Speaking to several attendees that day, we believed that most were interested in getting a jolt of the spirit, experiencing a miracle, or getting healed through the prayer of one of the high-profile leaders. The biblical exegesis was not the main draw.

Books, CDs, and DVDs were also promoted on stage, most of which were practical guides to experiencing the supernatural presence of God and bringing the "Culture of Heaven to Earth." In the lobby of the auditorium there were many books, CDs, and DVDs for sale, including recordings of all of the sessions at the conference. We bought a fourteen-CD set of all of the conference sessions, which was mailed a week later, at a cost of $80. The conference lasted four days and cost $125 per person. Access to a live web stream of the conference could be purchased for $50. The Ambassador Auditorium, which seats 1,262 people, was full for the duration of the event. It is not difficult to see how these registration fees, along with media sales, would be a major source of revenue for these groups.

In addition to direct revenue, these conferences raise the profile and enhance the legitimacy of the keynote speakers. This is important to note because it relates to the concept of "apostolic covering." If these leaders are seen to have the anointing of the Holy Spirit as apostles, then it is much more likely that other leaders and ministries will seek to be "aligned" with them under their covering. As we saw in Chapter 2, this has financial implications, as many leaders and organizations aligned with apostles will give money to the apostle or their organization as a way to confirm their allegiance with the apostle. Thus, the more high profile the apostle, the more organizations will align with him or her, and the more resources will flow to them and their ministries.

INTERNATIONAL HOUSE OF PRAYER

As mentioned in earlier chapters, IHOP consists of a megachurch—the 6,000-member Forerunner Christian Fellowship—along with IHOPU, a 24/7 prayer room, prophecy room, and healing room, all located in a converted suburban Kansas City shopping mall. IHOP also includes City of Hope, a facility near downtown Kansas City that includes dorm-like housing for homeless people. The sources of income for IHOP are quite different from those at Bethel. In our visit to Kansas City in 2013 to interview the IHOP leadership, they roughly broke down their income sources, as shown in Table 5.2.

Although the budget information we obtained from IHOP leaders is not precise, it nonetheless reveals several interesting facts about the group. First, like Bethel, only a small percentage (10 percent) of IHOP's annual income derives from plate donations from the group's megachurch. Second, like Bethel, a significant amount of income comes from media sales (books, CDs, DVDs, music) as well as from tuition from their ministry school.

Unlike Bethel, however, the highest percentage of IHOP's income (40 percent) comes from external donations. A senior leader at IHOP explained the matter this way:

> Respondent: Forty percent of our budget comes from general donations, people who believe in the cause.
> Interregator: Who believe in what you're doing.

Table 5.2 Sources of Income: IHOP Kansas City

Income Source	Percentage of Annual Budget
Plate Donations From Church	10
Staff Support Independently Raised	20
External Donations	40
IHOPU and Intern Tuition	15
Media Sales	15

Source: Interview with IHOP Leaders.

R: They believe it's immensely valuable that America has a place where you never stop praying.

I: Does that just come from everywhere?

R: Everywhere. We have a partnership program—people relate to us and partner with us. And you do know we have a Web stream that is serving 180 countries right now. Many people find that keeping that [prayer room] going serves the body of Christ. People get it on their phone, their computer, in their kitchen, their dorm room, their businesses, everywhere. They are connecting with us that way.

A number of IHOP leaders we interviewed explained how their web-based activities drove this external giving to the organization. Their website receives 26 million hits per year from all over the world. They have over 100 full-time people developing and delivering content for their website. The website contains a live stream of their 24/7 prayer room, which consists of constant prayer in musical format (prayers sung accompanied by an acoustic guitar, electronic keyboard, and drums). The website also contains a free video library of Mike Bickle's teaching, downloads of books by Bickle and other IHOP leaders, links to music downloads for purchase from seventeen different IHOP musicians and bands under the label of Forerunner Music, and advertising for IHOP conferences, ministries, internships, and IHOPU. According to their director of Information Technology (IT), the IHOP website draws about a million hours of watched video a month, which includes viewers from 180 nations. Thus, the IT director said, IHOP's is one of the top fifty websites in the world in terms of viewed hours of video content. They also do a daily show on GodTV, an international Charismatic TV channel. According to IHOP's leaders, these web-based media strategies drive the donations they receive from external sources—people who see what they are doing, particularly the emphasis on 24/7 prayer, and want to support it.

Several leaders we spoke with mentioned that IHOPU enrollment and visits to IHOP spiked after 2007, when they launched their live stream of the prayer room on the web. Another spike came in

2010–2011 when IHOP held a revival that was live-stream broadcast on their website. One senior leader explained these patterns this way:

> God kind of visited our student body, you can call it traditional revival, whatever. Lots of healings, new commitments. I think we had maybe 2,000 baptisms in that year . . . if you look behind me, there's a bunch of folders, these are all records from that period, that year, of all the different healings that year, according to body parts [laughter]. And that was shown on TV every night, all the different Christian media came around, and that was a big thing which spiked student numbers.

Clearly, IHOP has leveraged web-based media as their primary source of advertising and financing. IHOP's leadership team in the areas of technology and marketing are now looking to expand their already large presence on social media. Their Facebook page has over 260,000 followers, and, according to one marketing department leader, over 180,000 of those followers are "engaging," meaning that they are responding to posts, writing comments, and clicking on links to other content. According to this leader, those statistics represent an extremely high level of engagement compared with that of other Facebook pages of other Christian groups. Interestingly, the IHOP marketing department is now looking toward Facebook and other social media channels not as simply tools to get followers to come to IHOP events and programs, but rather as an end in itself—to disciple believers on social media platforms:

> On our page now, out of 267,000, we have 183,000 people engaging with us. That's well over 50 percent. There's no ministry that even approaches that, because we're using principles that really are relational and really working with people. The advertising we'll do is not to get them to an event; it's to get them to our Facebook page. Which is kind of a revolutionary concept of marketing. You're not trying to get them to buy a product; you're trying to get them to lock in with the relationship.

I'm hoping in the days ahead to build a huge evangelistic discipleship network through social media, reaching unbelievers and young people on Facebook, and treating it like it's its own nation. A lot of people say that, but how do you do those things I'm talking about? You actually target them through ads. You spend money on getting them the news feeds when you get them to a Facebook page that they could identify with.

Because IHOP is not building a traditional congregation, but rather a set of techniques and principles, they, like other INC groups, can not only advertise their product on the web, but deliver it as well.

One of the critical financial aspects of IHOP is that nearly all of its staff (700 full time and 300 part time) must raise their own financial support from a personal network of donors. This keeps staff overhead very low. In addition, IHOP employs over 3,000 interns who pay from $1,200 to $4,900 to participate in one of five different internship programs, each for a different time frame (three to six months) and each with a different emphasis. Each intern spends twenty-four hours a week in the prayer room praying and twenty-four hours a week in training for their internship role. *Most of the work at IHOP is undertaken by people whom IHOP does not directly pay—people who in fact pay IHOP for the privilege of serving the organization.*

Nontraditional Marketing and Finance in INC Christianity

These two cases highlight alternative methods of funding and marketing a religious group. Other INC groups have other ways of funding their operations that deviate from the traditional congregation-based ways of raising money. For example, Youth With a Mission (YWAM) relies almost exclusively on each participant's raising his or her own financial support from their own network of donors to pay for living expenses, tuition at YWAM Discipleship Training Schools, and trips related to mission and ministry. All INC groups share in common a low reliance on Sunday morning plate donations—which, as we previously noted, is still the dominant form of financing in most traditionally organized religious groups. In examining the various marketing and financing models of the INC groups in our study, we can sort them into the following four finance and marketing "tools." Some groups use all four tools; others use only one. Most use more than one.

I. The Web

INC Christianity seems particularly well positioned to take advantage of the expansion of web-based media as the foundation of both marketing and financing their activities for three reasons. First, INC spiritual practices produce visually compelling content that can be live streamed or recorded for consumption on the web. For example, ecstatic worship sessions with high-energy music and "signs and wonders"—including healing sessions, exorcisms, holy laughter, and people being "slain in the spirit"—make for interesting viewing, regardless of one's perspective on those practices. For true believers, free and easy access to content coming from the "epicenters" of revival around the world can produce excitement as well as commitment to leaders and ministries that may be located far from home.

Second, because INC leaders are less concerned with building congregations and institutions than they are with spreading particular practices—as well as their own perspectives and teachings—location becomes less of a constraint to growth, and the web can serve as the primary launching pad for their ministries. The cases of IHOP and Bethel illustrate this powerfully. IHOP is not concerned with building churches or communities, but rather with spreading the group's model of global 24/7 prayer to hasten the return of Jesus to earth. Thus the live web stream of IHOP's 24/7 prayer room serves as an easily replicable model for anyone on earth with an Internet connection. In fact, some prayer rooms around the world simply show the live stream on a screen, and worshipers gather to pray along with people in the live-streamed prayer room in Kansas City.

Similarly, Bethel is not concerned with franchising congregations or building a denomination, but rather with transmitting their "culture of heaven on earth." The web is a powerful tool for disseminating teachings of Bethel leaders through books, DVDs, and conference live streams, which demonstrates to followers from any religious tradition—or none at all—how to receive prophecies from God, pray for healing, deliver someone from a demonic oppression, or experience other manifestations of the Holy Spirit.

Third, the ideas of apostolic covering and "transferable anointing," also known as "impartation," are amenable to a web-based marketing strategy. If one is aligned with an apostle who is anointed by God with power and authority over the spiritual realm, then one has access to the same spiritual power to do great works—a notion of authority that allows for a "virtual" organizational strategy. If one simply has to be aligned with an apostle, rather than having to maintain close contact or an ongoing relationship, then that apostle can have a global following through the web, because the web facilitates the covering or impartation. The most striking example of this is Chuck Pierce, whom we discussed in Chapter 3. In addition to his 2,000-member Glory of Zion church in Corinth, Texas, Pierce has a much larger web-based following:

- 600 "Churches of Zion" meet in homes and watch live stream.
- 5,000 "Houses of Zion," individual households, watch live-stream church.
- 1,200 "Ministries of Zion" are 501(c)3 nonprofit organizations aligned with Chuck Pierce.
- 100 "Businesses of Zion" are aligned with Pierce.
- 60,000 individuals are on Pierce's e-mail list, to whom he sends daily encouragements and prophecies.

These web-based followers donate to Pierce's ministry as they would to a traditional congregation. In return they get the spiritual power that comes from being aligned with this apostle. As a result, the financial resources coming from Pierce's web-based following dwarf the resources he receives from plate donations at his megachurch.

2. THE PYRAMID

The idea of apostolic covering and the formation of a vertical network structure, as explained in Chapter 3, constitute a sort of multilevel marketing strategy. An apostle—Che Ahn or Peter Wagner, for example—oversees a group of apostles, who then oversee other groups of apostles, who then oversee a number of other ministries and churches. Recall that "spiritual covering" means power and authority flow down from the apostle, whereas financial support flows upward (and sometimes downward as well) along the pyramid. These multilevel vertical networks allow for much more expansive funding streams than would be possible in a single congregation. An apostle at the top of the pyramid receives donations from leaders and ministries that they may have very little contact with, thus multiplying their funding sources.

The pyramid also allows for heightened visibility and increased sales of books and other media from the apostle at the top of the pyramid, as well as increased registration at conferences where the head apostle is a marquee speaker. Leaders and ministries that are aligned with a particular apostle advertise and encourage their members to attend conferences when that apostles speaks, as well as purchasing books and other media created by the apostle.

3. THE CONFERENCE

Highly publicized conferences featuring well-known leaders, apostles, prophets, and worship bands are effective ways for INC leaders and ministries to market themselves to prospective followers. They also provide an important source of income for top-name speakers as well as their ministries. As previously mentioned, conferences account for $4 million in annual income for Bethel. Bill Johnson travels 120 days each year to speak at conferences and other events. At this writing, the Bethel website features Bill Johnson's schedule for the coming six months, including speaking engagements at sixteen different conferences in locations ranging from Atlanta, Georgia, to London, Australia, the Netherlands, and New Zealand. Bethel also holds several high-profile conferences at their own facility every year. Conference registration is typically between $90 and $200 per person.

Conferences are also a significant part of the recruiting strategy for IHOP. At this writing, IHOP has six different conferences listed on their website between March and September 2015, including conferences for high school students, African American believers, Chinese believers, and a children's ministry convening. IHOP's annual One Thing conference is the largest event—a four-day gathering that takes place after Christmas in downtown Kansas City's Convention Center and draws more than 25,000 participants. Popular Christian musicians, INC speakers, evangelists, and apostles are featured. The interns and students we spoke to at IHOP typically had their first live exposure to IHOP through a conference in Kansas City, which then led to them to associate with IHOP as interns or students.

Conferences offer a number of advantages as means of marketing and funding INC groups. First, there is very little overhead. Often, conferences will be held at auditoriums owned by one of the apostles in a network, so renting a facility is not necessary. Second, speakers in a particular network are often booked as a group, which maximizes the potential for attendance, thus exposing each network member to the other members' followers. This gives speakers legitimacy among the followers of others on the program and offers opportunities for sales of media that are sold at the conferences. Third, followers are drawn to the conferences in the hope of experiencing the miraculous, and they are willing to pay high registration fees for the possibility of receiving a miracle. The live experience of a conference is thus more potent than simply reading a book or watching a recording of the leaders' teachings on the Internet because the participant has a chance to experience firsthand the spiritual power of the leader by having the leader pray over, touch, or heal him or her. In our experience of attending INC conferences, the majority of participants were less interested in hearing the teaching or ideas of the speakers than they were in receiving a "jolt of the spirit" from being in the presence of apostles or being prayed for by them. We also met many participants whose first exposure to an INC leader or ministry was at a large, high-octane conference.

4. THE BOOT CAMP

Finally, the "ministry schools" or "universities" run by INC groups are powerful marketing tools to draw young adults. They offer an intensive "boot camp" experience in which participants live in close community with other young adults, follow intense schedules, work to meet rigorous requirements, and have opportunities to experiment in unorthodox ways with the supernatural.

IHOP's university courses and internship programs are probably the most rigorous of the INC experiences we examined. There are five types of internships provided by IHOP that are summarized in Table 5.3.

Young single interns are generally required to stay in dorm-like apartments provided by IHOP. They may not arrange their own accommodations and are not allowed to hold outside jobs or date during their internship. Interns' time is scheduled from 6 am to 10 pm, six days a week. The weekly schedule for the One Thing internship includes 35.5 hours spent praying, facilitating, and leading others in the 24/7 prayer room, 14.5 hours receiving teaching from IHOP leaders, 3 hours of outreach in the community, and 6 hours of "team

Table 5.3 Internship Programs: IHOP Kansas City

Internship	Ages/Marital Status	Length (Months)	Cost	Housing and Food
Intro to IHOPKC	All Ages Welcome	3	$1,200	Not Provided
Fire in the Night	18–30, Singles Only	3	$2,200	Provided
Hope City	18–40, Singles Only	3	$1,500	Provided
One Thing	18–25, Singles	6	$4,900	Provided

Source: IHOP Website.

building." As previously noted, internships cost participants from $1,200 to $4,900.

Bethel's BSSM is another example of a boot-camp-style program, although the schedule is somewhat more relaxed than IHOP's. Classes are held Monday through Thursdays from 1 pm to 4 pm and include high-intensity worship, sermons, and class time. Students read one book per week, usually a biography of a Pentecostal/Charismatic revivalist, and are required to write papers in response to the readings. Classes also consist of "revival groups" in which students learn to prophesy and pray for healing. Fridays are "activation" days when students go out into the Redding community and practice what they have learned during the week. Nighttime activities include small group meetings, "treasure hunts" (explained in Chapter 4), evangelism, and other public events.

YWAM, another INC group that is very popular among young adults, has communal "bases" around the world where young adults live, work, and eat together in a camp-like compound. One long-time YWAM member explains the allure of the boot camp environment:

> Here you instantly get serious. You have a lot of people that are just real serious, and there's worship sessions and Bible reading and class and lights-out, almost like a bit of a boot camp atmosphere, where they tell you when to sleep and when to eat. Really, exactly what I needed at the time, because I was just very undisciplined in those areas.

YWAM "missionaries" raise their own support to attend a five-month Discipleship Training School (DTS) at one of the YWAM bases, where they take twelve weeks of Bible classes, then an eight-week overseas mission trip. The first twelve-week period costs $3,200, which covers food, dorm-like housing at the YWAM base, and books. Students must then raise money for their eight-week mission trip, which varies in cost depending on the location. DTSs exist at YWAM bases all over the world. After completing this five-month program, students can apply to become YWAM staff. There are currently more than 18,000 staff members at YWAM. Like other INC groups, YWAM does not pay any of its staff members, including senior leaders. They must all raise support from their own personal network of donors.

The boot camp model has become so effective for INC groups that traditionally organized Pentecostal denominations are beginning to take notice and develop boot camps of their own. The Foursquare denomination, for example, has started a program called Ignite, a one-year training curriculum for young adults that mirrors YWAM. We interviewed one of the senior leaders of Ignite, and he explained the rationale for the creation of Ignite:

> YWAM has about 3 million missionaries over the years that have gone out.... So the concerns that I've heard over the years on these things, one is, as a local pastor you raise up this young person and then they go off with YWAM and they never come back, and you lose them. Ignite basically is a freshman year of Bible college, and couple that with other elements, so you pull in the missions element, you pull in the local church ministry element—the thread that keeps the whole thing together is discipleship immersion, the discipline. So we instituted curfew, which they said will never work today—most schools have done away with curfews. We put a curfew back in. We do mandatory devotions in the morning, so it's not just suggested or recommended. If you're not there at 8 am, we send somebody to your room to get you out of bed and bring you back. It's kind of a boot camp kind of thing. We do it for a full semester. No dating. We realize hormones being what they are, we're not saying you can't be interested in somebody, we're just saying, if you can't go three and a half minutes without having to hold their hand, something's wrong. We say no new tattoos, no new piercings. It's kind of an interesting thing, and it really just pulls everybody in.

The boot camp model seems to draw young adults because of its communal living situation, opportunities to participate in experimental and public ministries, the chance to travel, and—interestingly—its rigid rules and requirements. These young people seem to want an environment where they are pushed to the limit by "extreme" ministries, rigid schedules, and the high levels of commitment required. The programs are also typically short, from three to six months' duration. Requiring participants to maintaining their level of commitment to over longer periods of time would likely lead to increased dropouts or burnouts.

The boot camp model essentially funds itself. Not only do students and interns pay to live and take classes at the boot camp, but all of the staff members raise their own financial support as well. YWAM, IHOP, and BSSM staff for the most part raise their own money. Thus the only overhead costs these groups have are their property and buildings, which are funded by donations and the tuition that participants pay to participate.

Because these boot camps are short-term programs and frequently turn out new cohorts of trained evangelists, greater numbers of young people can be exposed to neo-Charismatic ministries and products than would be possible in a longer-term congregational ministry program. Even though the boot camp experience is short, these young people can become lifelong consumers of the web-based resources, media products, and conferences that these groups provide.

CONCLUSION

The network governance structure of INC groups allows them to market and fund themselves in unique ways. Because they are not primarily concerned with building congregations, they do not have to have a large amount of resources dedicated to staffing and managing programs internal to a congregation or ministry. Because their goal is promoting a way of living the Christian life rather than building a tight community of believers, they can go straight to the individual "customer" to teach him or her how to experience the supernatural and how to spread that knowledge to others.

The Tuesday night healing group at LA County-USC Medical Center, which we described in Chapter 4, is an illustrative example. These fifteen or so individuals come from different areas, different backgrounds, and different churches, if they attend church at all. But they all received their inspiration and learned the techniques to do their ministry from some combination of web-based content, DVDs, or conferences they had attended. Those who did belong to a church did not necessarily participate in an INC congregation, and those who did, did not seem as committed to their church as they did to the beliefs and experimental practices they learned from conferences and web-based resources. Thus INC Christianity is fundamentally a "practice" rather than a theology or way of building communities of believers. This practice can be learned through multiple methods and does not require membership in a congregation. In fact, it can be most effectively transferred through electronic media or intensive short-term teaching sessions in the form of conferences, ministry schools, or boot camps.

Thus resources can be devoted to expanding the "market" for these practices while reducing overhead costs associated with staffing and maintaining a day-to-day brick-and-mortar organization. Because web-based communication is cheap and has a worldwide reach, these organizations can increase their following at a low cost. Apostles can travel most of the year speaking at high-profile conferences and meeting with leaders who align with them and whom they "oversee," rather than spending time mentoring and teaching long-term congregation members. Boot camps can expand an apostle's following by turning over a new crop of students every three to six months. If IHOP has 3,000 interns coming for a three- to six-month internship, the numbers of followers IHOP can produce is exponentially higher than if they were ministering to the same congregational members year after year. In addition, charging tuition for the boot camp ensures a higher revenue stream than relying on the inclinations of a congregation to voluntarily put money in the donation plate at church, a revenue stream that has declined significantly in most churches over the years (Smith, Emerson, and Snell 2008).

In short, the typical congregation is a high-overhead, low-revenue stream model for a religious "firm." INC leaders have shifted toward a "pay-for-service" model in which followers pay for a particular product, whether it be a worship CD, a DVD of teachings, a boot camp program, apostolic covering, or conference registration. This model has two main advantages over the traditional brick-and-mortar church.

First, the number of paying "customers" can be expanded significantly beyond what would be possible in a single congregation. Second, more revenue can be generated because payment is required for most of the products offered (whereas denominationally affiliated churches offer most products for free, along with a plea for voluntary donations). Because of the potential it offers for greatly expanding the number of followers and increasing revenue, this model seems likely to continue to grow its "market share" compared with that of traditional religious congregations.

The shift from formal institutions to networks illustrates our theoretical argument that macrostructural change, including globalization and the digital revolution, allows global religious networks to develop that provide competitive advantages in the current religious marketplace. Digital communications technology empowers religious groups to expand their market share and their revenue streams well beyond their local communities. Of course, the expansion of the market for religious groups by using new communications technology is nothing new in history. The development of the printing press, for example, ended the Roman Catholic Church's monopoly on biblical interpretation and allowed various sects to grow internationally as Bibles and other literature were mass marketed over large geographic areas. The development of radio and television allowed evangelists and charismatic leaders to expand their following and revenue sources by instantaneously and directly appealing to a mass audience. The conference, rally, and revival meeting are also nothing new in religious history, nor are book and music sales.

What is different about this current movement, however, is that digital communications technology allows for virtual interactive networks to develop that can offer a substitute for the religious products that congregations and denominations have traditionally provided. In the pre-Internet era, for example, a religious celebrity such as Robert Schuller or Oral Roberts could offer a compelling product on television that replicated a church service for the viewer. These celebrities, although formally tied to denominations, operated independently, and certainly did not need their denominations for legitimacy or financial survival. They were, perhaps, prototypes of the independent apostles we highlight in this book.

Web-based technology, however, allows for the formation of networks on a larger scale and with a wider scope than is possible through a television-based ministry. First, the cost of producing Internet media is drastically lower than radio or television broadcast production costs. Anyone with a digital camera and an Internet connection can produce live-stream broadcasts. This lowers the barriers of entry to producing web-based media to almost nothing, allowing many more religious leaders into digital-media-based religious content. This creates more competition and requires religious leaders to have considerable charisma and compelling content to offer in order to rise above the noise.

Second, the Internet allows for 24/7 content delivery, including live streams available anytime, anywhere. Thus, any media product—including live video from a 24/7 prayer room, recordings from a conference, or a library of an apostle's teaching sessions—is available for download or live stream instantly at anytime or place. This considerably expands the types of content that can be delivered.

Third, the Internet allows for "pay-per-view" downloads, which increases the potential for revenue producing activity. Oral Roberts could ask for donations or advertise his latest book on his weekly TV program, but he could not require payment to watch the show. The Internet, however, allows for revenue-producing live streams of conferences and other video content. Revival Alliance conferences, for example, are available for live stream at a cost of $50.

Last, and perhaps most important, the Internet allows for interaction and communication between producers and consumers of content. Global Legacy, for example, allows members to view and connect with other Global Legacy members in their geographic area. Global Legacy also will facilitate miniconferences and meetings among members (for a fee) in particular areas. IHOP's Facebook page allows like-minded followers to connect with each other online as well as through the content that IHOP provides.

Although TV and radio communication allows for the expanded distribution of religious content to an audience much larger than a

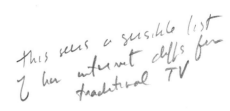

this seems a sensible list of her internet diffs from traditional TV

local congregation, *it does not facilitate the connection of viewers to each other in different locations.* The Internet, although not able to provide the rich relationships and sense of community that face-to-face connection over long periods of time can afford, does allow for virtual communities to emerge that bring together like-minded fellow travelers. For some believers, this possibility mitigates the need to involve themselves in a local religious community at all. Money, loyalty, and communication thus flow not just from follower to leader and back, but horizontally among nodes in the network.

Noticeably absent in most of these far-flung networks is the likelihood of building long-lasting institutions that could have a sustained social impact on local communities. We explore these and other potential weakness of the network form of organization in the next chapter.

CHAPTER SIX

COMPETITIVE
DISADVANTAGES
AND DOWNSIDES

The previous chapters documented the advantages of INC Christianity in the current religious marketplace. This chapter addresses the weaknesses of INC Christianity and its disadvantages when compared with religious groups that are organized around traditional congregations and denominations. Paradoxically, these disadvantages are primarily a result of the source of its central advantages: its network structure of governance. Although we predict that INC Christianity will continue to gain market share in the global religious economy, these weaknesses likely will limit INC growth and at least partially prevent it from becoming the "transformative" religious movement that its proponents claim it to be.

OVERSELLING THE MIRACULOUS

The primary distinction of Pentecostal/Charismatic Christianity has always been its emphasis on direct contact with the supernatural in the form of miraculous "signs and wonders" such as glossolalia (speaking in tongues), supernatural healing, exorcism, and direct communication from God through prophecy. The "product cycle" of Pentecostal/Charismatic groups, as described in Chapter 2, tends to follow a consistent pattern:

1) The emergence of a leader with the ability to produce miraculous signs and wonders who breaks away from constraints imposed by traditionally organized denominational congregations.

2) The rapid growth in the number of followers that is due to the leader's experimentation with direct contact with supernatural forces and other miraculous phenomena.

3) Controversy and criticism resulting from innovation and experimentation on the part of leaders and participants in the movement.

4) An attempt to routinize and regulate practices of the supernatural and miraculous in response to controversy.

5) The emergence of new charismatic leaders who leave the routinizing movement to escape growing institutional constraints.

It remains to be seen whether INC Christianity is simply a network of new leaders in Stage 5 who will eventually routinize and create denomination-like structures as their groups mature and continue to grow and when they inevitably face controversy and criticism over their practices. If, however, the network structure of INC Christianity allows for an escape from this cycle of routinization, it could be that INC leaders will not have to eventually institutionalize their beliefs and practices, and relatively unregulated experimentation can continue indefinitely. If we assume that this is the case, INC leaders can continue to operate and experiment in the realm of the supernatural without regulation or oversight.

Inherent in this unregulated environment is a tendency to overstate and oversell experiences with the miraculous. The greater the claims a leader makes to have special revelations from God—or to be an agent of "social transformation," complete with the elimination of crime, disease, poverty, and suffering—the more likely people will be attracted to the leader, but also the more likely they will eventually be disappointed over time when those outcomes fall short of expectations. It seems, for example, that the majority of those who were prayed for at the LA County-USC Medical Center emergency room were not immediately and completely healed, yet the practitioners hold a strong belief that "God wants to heal everyone" and that "all who ask will be healed." It is likely that this belief is not sustainable over the long term in the face of mounting evidence that, in fact, not everyone who asks for healing is healed.

It is also extremely likely that at least some of the specific revelations of anointed prophets will turn out to be false. Although it is possible to continue to grow by convincing new believers of "oversold" claims of supernatural intervention, overselling also creates disillusioned customers over time who might eventually leave for religious groups making more modest claims or abandon organized religion altogether.

This seems to have happened with the Kansas City Prophets in their break with the Vineyard. Vineyard leaders expressed concern that Mike Bickle and others who traveled with John Wimber in the 1990s were "overreaching" in their prophecies about world events, which were "almost always wrong." Followers, however, seem to be fairly forgiving when prophets get things wrong. Calvary Chapel founder Chuck Smith, for example, predicted that Jesus would return in the year 1981. Despite the year 1981 coming and going fairly uneventfully, Chuck Smith continued to lead the thriving Calvary Chapel movement for another 30 years. He did not continue making bold prophetic predictions, however.

Current large-scale prophecies from multiple INC leaders that seem fairly unlikely to take place any time soon include the following:

1) The transfer of wealth to Christian believers on a worldwide scale never seen before in history.
2) A massive number of new converts to the Christian faith in the United States, starting in California.
3) The rise of "kingdom-minded" (meaning socially conservative "born-again") Christian believers to the top positions in government, education, media, arts, entertainment, and business.
4) Jesus coming back to earth soon to rule the world.

No concrete dates are associated with these predictions—therefore their lack of fulfillment can always be explained by the prophesier's claiming that they will be fulfilled at some time in the future. However, the longer these predictions go unfulfilled, it seems the more difficult it will become to keep people from skepticism about large-scale prophecies like these and the people who make them.

Most smaller-scale prophecies coming from INC prophets have a vague, nonfalsifiable quality about them that allow them to be confirmed by a number of different outcomes. However, a lack of fulfilled prophecies may leave some disillusioned over time. For example, prophet Cindy Jacobs publishes a list of prophecies called the "Word of the Lord" on her website. These prophesies were available on her Generals International website for 2015:

The Church

We are now in the Jesus People Movement that has been prophesied about for years. The great harvest of souls is now upon us, and with it, another Great Awakening.

Israel

This is the time for the harvest of the Jews to begin. Bold witness will arise from believers in both the Jewish and Arab sectors.

United States

The Lord is going to use the coming shakings, even from more internal attacks, to wake up people to their need for God. This will come seemingly in waves, subside, and come again. Christians will boldly start giving testimony of their Christian faith and be very counter-cultural. More producers will make movies with godly values, and Hollywood will start to lose money on the "dark field" as the appetite of the nation changes.

Canada

Canada is going to be a key missions force to reach those who are in ISIS and radical Islam.

Latin America

Communism will start to lose its grip in Latin America. The people of Latin America will start to shift the trend from hard leftist ideology to more moderate forms of government.

Europe

Europe will experience a financial shaking and this will affect the U.S. economy, though not at the level of the 2008 economic meltdown. This may or may not happen in the Fall of 2015, depending upon people's prayers, but will eventually happen. In the midst of this, the re-evangelization of Europe will begin. God is listening to the prayers of those in Europe who are shaken and distressed, and He is preparing to answer.

It is easy to see why these prophecies would be encouraging to Christian believers and motivate them to practice their faith boldly, but it also seems that if these prophecies were wrong it would lead at least some to question Jacobs's prophetic credentials. The Latin American prophecy seems wrong from the outset, as communism has not had a strong presence in Latin America for decades. And if Europe does not experience a financial collapse of some kind in 2015 (it has not), it seems that some would question her prophetic credentials. However, there is a disclaimer built into that prophecy: She states that the financial crisis could be avoided, depending on people's prayers. So if it does not occur, it could be explained as a victory—the prayers of the people of God saved Europe from the collapse.

Although none of these prophecies are falsifiable—that is, none can be disproved by disconfirming evidence—they seem likely to disillusion some followers at some point if they do not eventually come to pass. The more outrageous prophecies also seem likely to be off-putting to newcomers to the faith, which may limit the growth potential of the movement.

In addition to the limited shelf life of over-the-top prophesying, the excitement created by ecstatic worship and manifestations of the Spirit such as holy laughter, shaking, crying, and being slain in the Spirit also seems difficult to sustain over time. Kaitlyn Crosby, whom we met in Chapter 3, admits that the allure of these types of experiences eventually begins to fade:

> When people experience the presence of God for the first time, if they've had a fresh encounter with God, that creates so much hype, so much

excitement that's really real, but the truth is that your life with God is not this one mountaintop experience. There's a lot of lows and a lot of dark nights. So the hype gets generated with really experiencing the presence of God, and then people come back and they keep expecting that, and sometimes that's not how God wants to show up, so that can be disappointing for people and that can cause a lot of disillusionment.

Specifically, Kaitlyn said that many people eventually tire of the "hype" that gets generated around the miraculous at INC conferences.

We met numerous young people, however, who keep the hype and excitement going by bouncing from one INC conference or "boot camp" to another. Many of the participants we interviewed had been to multiple conferences and ministry training programs held by several different INC groups. The most commonly attended events were those hosted by IHOP in Kansas City, Bethel in Redding, and YWAM, the group's various bases.

One of the young women we interviewed described this as a "revolving door," shuttling participants from one INC group to another:

One of my housemates went to IHOP, and during the school she was doing stuff with YWAM and getting credit for her major for journalism, because she's been doing journalism stuff for the [YWAM evangelistic ministry]. And she was road-tripping up to Bethel over spring break. And some people leave college altogether and get into it. I had a friend who was also my housemate. She was supposed to graduate this spring. She felt like she was supposed to go to YWAM in Hawaii, so she left college and went and did six months of YWAM and now she's back and she'll be finishing college in the fall.

Although these exciting experiences may hold young peoples' attention for a number of years, they do not seem economically sustainable, even if they are emotionally sustainable, over time. Because payment is required for these conferences, training schools, and internships, young people must raise support to attend them through their own network of donors. It seems unlikely that many of donors would want to continue to support these ventures indefinitely. Thus, INC groups that are made up primarily of young people must constantly recruit new participants, as it is likely that many will eventually age out and join more traditional groups.

One of our respondents commented on the relative lack of middle-aged and older people at many INC events and meetings:

> Maybe when people mature and they want to settle down, they'll get involved in places like [denominational congregation], but it doesn't offer the same kind of hype that a lot of Charismatic ministries do. So I think a lot of people stay in areas where they're getting that sort of energy. There are some older people in Houses of Prayer and sometimes you feel like, "What are you still doing here?"

This statement reflects an expectation that many people will cycle out of these programs once they obtain stable jobs and start families, making it difficult to sustain the excitement of traveling the conference and training school circuit. This limits the growth potential of these groups if the majority of their following is in one particular age demographic.

Lack of Stable Community

Sociologists of religion tell us that the "products" that many people are seeking when they join a religious group are meaning and belonging (Smith et al. 1998; Berger 1967; Emerson and Smith 2000). As Emerson and Smith (2000) state, "Religion is, by its very nature, a central source of the types of morally orienting collective identities that provide people with meaning and belonging."

INC Christianity provides meaning in compelling ways. Being involved in a supernatural battle on which the fate of the universe depends and bringing heaven to earth by accessing the supernatural power of the Holy Spirit create a strong narrative of meaning in which to participate. Some INC groups provide a compelling environment of belonging as well, particularly through communal living in boot camps for young people. However, it seems that INC groups are weak in offering long-term stable communities in which to find belonging.

INC Christianity, as we have described elsewhere, is mainly concerned with promoting a set of practices as a means of connecting with the divine and experiencing the supernatural. As a result, these groups focus their energy and resources on spreading information and training on how to pray for healing, receive words from God, deliver someone from demonic influence, pray for a nation's revival, and wage spiritual warfare against territorial spirits. They are not primarily concerned with building congregations that can serve as long-term communities for individuals who are searching for a deeply rooted sense of belonging.

Some of the senior leaders we interviewed recognized this weakness. One leader of IHOP expressed a desire among IHOP's leadership to focus more energy on building a community:

This is known as a house of prayer. A house of prayer is a place to pray. Even though we have all the ingredients that look like a local congregation and local church, we never emphasize the dimension of the church life. Coming to Sunday morning is like attending a weekend conference. You can sit there. There's no small groups. You might be attending our church. There's no membership roll. You get healing. You get touched by the message, you love the worship. But in terms of community development, connecting with people, it's all organic with no deliberate organization. It's not structured.

Not only must we build the house of prayer foundation, which has been established now for 14 years, the prayer room is pretty stable, not the strongest, it can go stronger, but I think we had to now focus on the development of the church life, because many people are not called to be full-time intercessory missionaries like us. They're called to just come on a weekend and work in the marketplace. We have not given them the due attention, because what we're called to do was a very focused assignment of building an unceasing altar of adoration, intercession, and worship.

This quotation highlights the difficulty of combining a narrowly focused, practice-oriented ministry with the building of a stable, long-term community that satisfies the need for belonging. Although participants may be drawn to the excitement of 24/7 prayer for the evangelization of the world and the return of Jesus, it does not seem likely that people will stay committed over years or decades in the absence of a sense that they are part of a community. A number of our respondents observed that few people remain involved in houses of prayer once they get older, have families, and find stable jobs.

Some, however, become leaders and staff at the boot camps and ministry schools as they get older and have families, because of the camaraderie and excitement of boot-camp-type environments. This, however, is a difficult life because most of these leaders and staff have to raise their own financial support. A leader of YWAM programs described the financial risks of living on a YWAM base while raising a family:

There's a bit of recklessness about a lot of us. If some people saw how I run my finances with three kids, they go, "You're out of your mind." You know what? I am, but I really believe that this is what the Lord has for us right now. Really, I've been going month-to-month with little kids, where you don't have anything in savings. God is your plan B. There's a lot of us here on this campus who live that way. That's a huge challenge, and in YWAM, probably a thousand of those people retiring in the next 10 years, they're like "What do we get to do? Where's our place in missions?" Because they didn't save for retirement. They don't have a backup plan. YWAM is their tribe. So it's going to be a bunch of seniors hanging around here on our bases and some of them may become incapacitated eventually physically, and what are we going to do? That's a very real challenge. We're not set up for long-term care. We're also not a welfare place. So it's got some interesting challenges, because they're YWAMers.

Most of the INC ministries that do offer tight-knit communities and a sense of belonging are mainly boot camps and training schools set up primarily for young people. Those who choose to stay throughout their lives do so at considerable cost. Most INC groups, however—including HROCK, Bethel, and IHOP—offer a traditional congregation with Sunday services. Still, these congregations are oriented toward learning practices related to the supernatural rather than building a stable, long-term community. Their relative weakness in being able to provide a sense of belonging therefore seems likely to limit the growth potential of INC groups, particularly among cohorts of middle-agers and older adults.

CAPACITY FOR LONG-TERM SOCIAL CHANGE

As we explored in Chapter 4, one of the primary attractions of INC Christianity, particularly among young people, is the narrative of social transformation. INC leaders have provided a compelling vision for "bringing heaven to earth" through supernatural means. In our travels and interviews, the theme of transforming the "seven mountains of culture"—government, business, arts and entertainment, media, education, religion, and the family—came up constantly as the means by which God will establish heaven on earth through those who believe in Him.

Although the prospect of being part of such a grand, supernaturally driven world transformation inarguably generates excitement and passion among INC believers (there is reason to believe that this wholesale transformation will not happen) Prophecy, intercessory prayer, and spiritual warfare are the main tactics that INC groups use to pursue their transformative agenda of world transformation—supernatural interventions that seem unreliable, even if they sometimes appear to be demonstrably real.

The "Transformations" video series created by INC leader George Otis Jr. purports to document cases of transformation in cities and nations all over the world, including Cali, Colombia; Kiambu, Kenya; Hemet, California; and Alomlonga, Guatemala. Prayer rallies and strategic spiritual warfare, rather than institutional reform, are given credit in these videos for falling crime and poverty rates, the elimination of government corruption, and other positive social outcomes.

The primary goal of Radiance International in Hollywood is the transformation of the entertainment industry to reflect godly values. Their strategy to achieve that goal is to establish a 24/7 prayer house on the Sunset Strip, as well as to develop local talent through an art gallery and recording studio. HROCK in Pasadena is developing relationships with artists and media firms through the use of their facility and by promoting the "market" for Christian films among Hollywood producers. None of these undertakings seem likely to alter the dynamics of the entertainment industry in any significant ways.

Supernatural interventions aside, the efforts INC groups to transform society seem likely to be hindered by what we have described in this book as its primary competitive advantage—its network structure. The lack of long-term institutional infrastructure and organizational capacity limits the ability of INC Christianity to effect long-term social change. Networks of individuals can collaborate together for short-term tasks such as prayer rallies and conferences, but they are less able than formal organizations to influence the large-scale institutions that control the seven mountains of culture. Consider the mountain of government as an example.

The most publicized forays into the political arena among INC groups have taken the form of large prayer rallies and religio-political networks. As mentioned earlier, the Response prayer rallies headlined by Rick Perry and Bobby Jindal are instructive examples of this phenomenon. A significant number of INC leaders mobilized to organize these rallies, and Perry's rally in Houston, by all measures, was a success, with more than 30,000 attendees. This did not, however, advance Perry's presidential campaign among the broader populace.

Contrast that outcome to the efforts of more organizationally sophisticated conservative Christian groups such as Focus on the Family and its offshoot, the Family Research Council, Ralph Reed's Faith and Freedom Coalition, Concerned Women of America, and the Southern Baptists' Ethics and Religious Liberty Commission. These groups have influenced and even shaped the Republican Party through years of fund-raising, getting voters to the polls, filing lawsuits to influence policy, and staffing positions in local and state GOP party offices. These groups sponsor events like the Values Voter Summit, which most aspiring Republican presidential candidates attend to gain the endorsement of these groups. Republican candidates openly court the endorsements of Christian Right leaders such as James Dobson and Ralph Reed.

In fact, it is difficult for a Republican to win the nomination for president if these groups openly oppose their candidacy, although Donald Trump seems to be the exception to that general rule. The power of these organizations within the Republican Party is felt at every level; according to some analysts, that intensity of influence has created a "civil war" within the GOP between evangelical "values voters" focused on social issues such as abortion and gay marriage and the probusiness wing of the party, which is more moderate on controversial social issues (Schnabel 2013; Keckler and Rozell 2015).

In contrast, INC groups have few institutional mechanisms to leverage influence in the area of government. Apostles may "pray over" prominent politicians, as apostle Thomas Muthee did for Sarah Palin and as Lou Engle did for Newt Gingrich— and Lance Wallnau for Donald Trump. They may also organize prayer rallies as the springboard for their campaigns, but their influence beyond those events seems limited because as networks focused almost exclusively on teachings about ecstatic experiences and prayer, they have little institutional leverage to command the political sphere, where influence comes from the ability to produce money and votes for candidates. One exception is the use of prayer networks during election time to activate voters around a particular candidate or issue. Cindy Jacobs, for example published a "prayer guide" during the 2012 presidential election through her United States Reformation Prayer Network, which gave followers a list of outcomes to pray for regarding issues and candidates during the run-up to the election. As of yet, she has not released a similar prayer guide for the 2016 election.

This undoubtedly swayed those in the prayer network as to how to vote. But generally INC Christians are not known (or at least not known yet) for having the ability to deliver votes or raise money to a degree that would allow them to influence policy at the national level. It remains unlikely, for example, that Bickle's endorsement of Ted Cruz made much of a difference in Cruz's electability.

Overall, the worldview of INC Christianity works against its developing the kind of institutional power and influence that would allow leaders in the movement to gain dominion over the seven mountains of culture. Their operating assumption is that the most important realm is the unseen spiritual domain, where "principalities and powers" influence events on earth to a much greater extent than do "on-the-ground" institutions. Thus, establishing 24/7 houses of prayer or pursuing strategic-level spiritual warfare against demonic territorial spirits is, in the eyes of INC Christians, much more likely to produce transformative results on the ground than working year after year to build institutional capacity (think tanks to craft policy proposals, for example) to influence elections.

Instead, INC leaders focus on getting direct words from God through prophesies, then on praying for the outcomes revealed in those prophecies. As mentioned earlier, one prophecy that has become accepted among many INC apostles and prophets is the idea that there will be a massive transfer of wealth to kingdom-minded believers through the business sector. They teach that, once this transfer of wealth happens, it can be mobilized to transform the other sectors. In the meantime, they pray and wait for this transfer to happen rather than build the institutional capacity to grow influence the seven mountains of culture through more mainstream means.

In addition to the lack of institutional capacity to influence the various sectors of society, the theology of INC Christianity lacks a clear vision for what social transformation should look like even if INC groups were to gain influence. In INC writings about social transformation, authors cite the elimination of poverty, crime, corruption, and other social ills as signs of transformation, but they have no clear policy agenda as to how to produce these outcomes. Thus INC Christianity has no clear policy agenda, other than the usual Christian Right moral issues of opposing abortion and gay marriage and seeking to establish prayer in the public schools. Because they see the cause of social ills as spiritual, rather than structural, it makes sense they would not have a poverty-reduction policy agenda, for example, other than putting kingdom-minded, spirit-filled believers at the top of the mountains of business and government, which would then allow God's spiritual and material blessing to flow into society through them.

The INC literature on social transformation is therefore focused on identifying and empowering "workplace apostles" who can usher in social transformation, rather than on the policies that these apostles should implement once they rise to the top of a particular mountain. Because they are apostles, it is believed, they will know what to do when they get there because they will have direct access to God. And the way that apostles are identified in their various sectors is simply their success in rising to the top of that sector. C. Peter Wagner, in his book *Apostles Today* (2010), states that the way you recognize workplace apostles is by the amount of respect, money, and influence they command:

> People will recognize the authority of a workplace apostle if they command respect from associates and if their track record authenticates their effectiveness in their field of endeavor.... Although it is not the only consideration, money is one of the major factors commanding respect in the workplace. Access to financial resources builds credibility and confers authority more in the workplace than in the church.... Authority also comes from the unusual influence one has earned in his or her determined sphere of the workplace (Wagner 2010:115–117).

According to Wagner, however, mere success in one's field does not by itself qualify one to be a workplace apostle. An apostle must also use his or her authority to promote godly values in their sphere of influence:

> Not every financially successful Christian leader in the workplace is necessarily an apostle. Those who are apostles, however, will have a Kingdom mentality—meaning that their driving passion is to see God's kingdom values permeate society on every level (Wagner 2006:117).

Statements like this abound in INC literature on social transformation. In our review of this literature, however, we have found almost nothing that delineates what those kingdom values are and what a society would look like in which "kingdom values permeate society on every level."

To summarize, the flexibility and innovation that comes with being organized as a network of Charismatic individual leaders may come at the cost of the ability to effect long-term social change. This would not be a problem if the goal of INC Christianity were simply to gain converts and prepare them for the next life. But their own theology places central importance on social transformation and bringing heaven to earth in the here and now. Yet the lack of institutional capacity from its network structure seems to limit the possibility of achieving of this goal. In addition, the absence of a clear vision of what kind of social transformation is desired, and what a "godly" society would look like—other than having kingdom-minded believers controlling it—seems to doom this project from the outset.

The lack of clear vision for social transformation is also related to INC Christianity's network structure. A network of dynamic entrepreneurial leaders averse to creating formal organizations is incapable of producing the types of institutional governance structures and think tanks that would allow for the construction of a coherent vision of a "good society." In addition, many of the most dynamic and popular leaders of this movement lack a postsecondary education and therefore should not be expected to have a coherent vision of social change and of how to promote it. The supernatural worldview of its adherents also reinforces the lack of a clear vision for social change—because God directly speaks to his anointed apostles and prophets, one does not need a blueprint produced according to the logic of complex human societies to transform them. One must simply listen to God's voice and implement His requests and pray against the demonic forces that would prevent the implementation of those requests. From a purely secular sociological perspective, the kinds of widespread social change that these groups desire to foster seem unlikely to be realized. This would not be as much of a competitive disadvantage if it were not the case that wholesale "social transformation" is being sold as one of the primary purposes of the entire INC enterprise.

CORRUPTION AND SCANDAL

The networks of INC Christianity also seem more vulnerable to scandal and corruption than traditionally organized congregations and denominations because of its relative lack of accountability structures and the tremendous amount of authority and autonomy given to dynamic, high-profile individual leaders. Traditionally organized religious groups are, of course, no stranger to scandal and corruption. One need only look at the recent sexual abuse scandal in the Catholic Church, one of the most bureaucratically complex religious groups in the world, to see that scandal and corruption can occur in any organizational setting. Yet INC Christianity seems particularly fertile ground for financial excesses and abuses of power.

We were told repeatedly in our interviews that prophets, apostles, and other transformative leaders should not be hindered in their use of money by boards, councils, denominations, and other oversight bodies. Given the amount of money that the network structure can produce from numerous sources and the high status afforded to apostles and prophets, this lack of oversight seems to be an invitation to venality among high-profile leaders.

The vertical network structure that we described in Chapter 3 allows for a multilevel financial organization in which apostles receive money from leaders, churches, and other ministries that want to be aligned with that apostle, without that apostle having much, if any, direct contact with those groups that support him or her financially. Followers seem happy to support that apostle, as long as the promise of spiritual power flowing from the apostle remains.

This alignment arrangement means that well-known prophets, apostles, and other leaders are able to develop networks of financial support that are far wider than would be possible if their support were limited to followers they actually came in contact with directly. In addition, their position as apostles allows them to make all decisions about how that money is used, without challenge by any oversight board. Although most leaders and their ministries have boards to maintain their nonprofit status, it is clear that if an apostle thinks a particular course of action is what God wants, there is rarely any resistance to that declaration from the board. In addition, the teachings of these leaders generally argue that wealth is unequivocally a blessing from God and should be seen as a sign of anointing rather than feared or critiqued. According to one of the INC leaders we interviewed,

> The people that have the influence are the successful people. And in most cases success is tied to wealth. Influential people have wealth. So there is a strong teaching that it is the will of God that kingdom-minded people get rich, control large amounts of money and influence.

Thus, having access to wealth is seen as evidence of being an apostle and the key to influencing the world for God. In fact, as previously mentioned, one of the key claims of influential prophets in this movement is that there will be a massive transfer of wealth to kingdom-minded leaders who will use that wealth to bring God's kingdom to earth. C. Peter Wagner, in his (2010) autobiography, states:

> I think that it is time we began agreeing strongly and openly that we cannot expect to be agents in God's hands for massive and sustained reformation unless we control huge amounts of wealth. In all of human history, three things, above all others, have changed society: violence, knowledge, and wealth. And the greatest of these is wealth!

This theology makes internal critiques and/or regulation of the financial practices of INC leaders difficult. If wealth is a prerequisite for being an agent of social transformation in God's hands, it becomes difficult to criticize an apostle for accumulating wealth. This then raises the likelihood that these leaders may misuse financial resources gained from their followers.

The network structure of INC leadership apostles, along with a general lack of organizational oversight, can also be fertile ground for other types of scandals among high-profile leaders–apostles and prophets. Although there is no shortage of scandal within traditionally organized religious groups, the lack of oversight and accountability in the INC Christianity network structure provides less disincentive for scandal and corruption than could be provided by a conscientiously managed denominational structure. The high-profile scandal of INC evangelist Todd Bentley provides an instructive example.

Bentley grew up in British Columbia, Canada, and converted to Christianity in his teens after a troubled home environment led him to drug addiction and eventually time in prison. Soon after his conversion, he began an evangelistic ministry. In 1998, at age 22, he became the leader of Fresh Fire Ministries, which he still currently leads. The purpose of Fresh Fire is to evangelize by holding revival meetings that emphasize the power of the Holy Spirit all over the world. On April 2, 2008, Bentley was invited to lead a one-week revival meeting in Lakeland, Florida, hosted by Stephen Strader, the local pastor of the Ignited Church (McMullen 2008). The meetings quickly grew to 10,000 attendees a night and ended up lasting until August of that year. The revival was live streamed over the Internet and broadcast live on GodTV. Forty-five days into the event, the live-stream website had received over a million hits (Geivett and Pivec 2014). This became known as the "Florida Outpouring," and many accounts of miraculous healing were reported, along with other manifestations of the Holy Spirit, such as people in the congregation being "slain in the Spirit."

In the midst of the outpouring, in June of 2008, Bentley agreed to become aligned with apostles Che Ahn, Bill Johnson, and John Arnott. Under the leadership of Peter Wagner, Bentley was officially commissioned as an evangelist under the authority of these apostles in a ceremony that was broadcast on GodTV (Geivett and Pivec 2014). Soon after this alignment, on July 9, 2008, ABC News Nightline broadcast a critical investigation of Bentley's ministry, finances, and criminal past. On July 23, Bentley announced that he would no longer be leading the revival meetings in Lakeland and resigned from Fresh Fire, his original ministry. It was later revealed that he had an inappropriate relationship with one of his female staff members and was struggling with alcohol abuse. The "outpouring" ended soon after Bentley's departure.

After these revelations emerged, Bentley lost his official alignment with Ahn, Johnson, and Arnott. They all agreed to serve in an advisory role during Bentley's "restoration" process. Arnott stated in a *Charisma* magazine article (Gaines 2009), "Relationally we all do care for him. But he wouldn't be seen as a member in good standing." Bentley then aligned himself with Rick Joyner, another apostle, and moved to Fort Mill, North Carolina, to take a place in Joyner's ministry. Bentley reestablished his ministry under the name Fresh Fire USA after his move to Fort Mill, divorced his wife, and married the staff member with whom he had had an affair. In the same 2009 *Charisma* article, Joyner stated, "The whole point of restoration is to get you back from where you were. He is going to be back in ministry, and we want to lay a solid foundation for that. There are partners who want to support his process. They want him restored and healthy. It's just building and infrastructure" (Gaines 2009). In 2010, less than two years after the scandal broke, Bentley was "restored" and returned to preaching and leading crusades. His popularity has never returned to the peak of his Florida Outpouring, but he continues to have a following and speaks at conferences and events.

Again, scandals such as this are nothing new in religious groups and therefore not unique to INC Christianity. What is instructive about this case, however, is the flexibility and speed with which Bentley was able to shift from one apostolic alignment to another to reboot his ministry. In a period of less than two years, Bentley's affair and substance abuse issues were revealed, he stepped down from his ministry, remarried, after which he was restored to ministry under a new apostolic alignment, and created a new organization under the name of his founding ministry. In a more traditionally organized congregation or denomination, a person involved in a scandal such as this might be restored to ministry eventually, but the process would likely take much longer and involve more sanctions and various other requirements to reduce the chances of recidivism. But as we previously asserted, religious networks composed of wealthy, high-profile charismatic evangelists with little or no oversight provide fewer disincentives for scandalous behavior among its leaders.

Another instructive aspect of Bentley's scandal is that it illustrates the lower costs of a scandal involving leaders in a network. Although Todd Bentley never regained a following as large as the one he attracted during the Florida Outpouring, those who left his original flock were able to seamlessly join the following of another apostle. Also, the apostles with whom he had been associated—including Che Ahn, Bill Johnson, and John Arnott—did not suffer any loss of credibility or support, because their relationships with Bentley were loose and informal. He was not officially part of any of their ministries.

It is possible that some whose devotion to INC Christianity was sparked during the Florida Outpouring were disillusioned enough after Bentley's scandal to leave INC Christianity altogether. But it seems likely that most of them simply shifted their allegiance from Bentley to another leader in the INC network.

This case illustrates that, despite the lower levels of accountability and the seemingly high risk of scandal, dramas like the Bentley scandal, and the whiff of corruption, may be less threatening to the network structure as a whole than would be the case with a more traditional denominational bureaucracy. When one leader and his followers drop out of the network because of scandal, the network as a whole is less strongly affected than when scandal infects a large denominational–bureaucratic organization, as we have seen with sex scandals in the Catholic Church.

Even though the network structure seems to allow a greater possibility for corruption and scandal, it also lessens the damage to the basic web of relationships that comprise the network as a whole. The total body of followers that sustains the network is negligibly diminished by disaffected dropouts, who can easily find the same kind of charismatic leadership in the congregation of another leader in the network. Still, one might reasonably assume that at least a few of the followers of a leader involved in scandal and corruption would seek other modes of living a life of faith and not another leader in the same mold.

The Weaknesses of Strengths

To summarize, all four of the weaknesses that we have identified here are products of the primary competitive strength of INC Christianity: its network structure. The network structure allows charismatic leaders to experiment with ways of engaging the supernatural without the potential burden of denominational oversight. This creates fertile ground for spontaneous innovations that attract large followings, but also produces extreme, often outlandish, beliefs and proclamations that are likely to disillusion followers over time when the product does not deliver its consumers all that has been promised.

The network structure also allows for the pursuit of novel techniques for accessing the supernatural, but this often comes at the expense of more mundane tasks, such as creating time and space to nurture stable, long-term relationships among believers to develop over time. The church potluck, holiday social, and weekly Bible study are replaced by "treasure hunts," revivals, and 24/7 prayer. Although in comparison, the former may seem dull and workaday they also provide the context for the development of close, long-term relationships that give members a sense of stability and belonging. They also can be mobilized to bring emotional, logistical, and material help during life's many crises. INC groups' aggressive appeal to young people, coupled with INC leaders' constant search for new techniques to spark the next outpouring of the Spirit, deters the formation of the kind of long-term interpersonal bonds that create stability and provide a sense of belonging—two of the key benefits of more formally institutionalized religious movements.

The network structure of INC Christianity allows dynamic entrepreneurial leaders to combine and recombine their efforts on short-term projects such as conferences, prayer rallies, and revival meetings. These networks do not provide the institutional support, however, to foster a theologically systemized vision of social change or the institutional capacity to effect reform in the sectors of society that INC groups so desperately want to see changed. The Catholic Church, by contrast, has a rich theology in the areas of social justice and transformation, as well as universities, think tanks, and lobbying groups that are able to influence social ethics and public policy in measurable ways.

Finally, the network structure allows high-profile leaders the autonomy to devise their own strategies, mobilize their own resources, and lead their followers as they see fit, without hindrance from regulatory agents and structures. Although this can foster innovative rituals and practices, it can also more easily lead to corruption, scandal, and the potential for the exploitation of the followers of these religious entrepreneurs.

Strictly in terms of growth potential, these weaknesses are outweighed by the advantages provided by unleashing the energy and charisma of dynamic leaders without restraint, along with the ability to collaborate with other popular leaders while keeping overhead low. But the long-term appeal of the religious product that this form of Christianity offers is diminished by its inattention to social structures that help to create a sense of belonging and community and to focus the energy of the group in a way that tangibly and reliably influences long-term social change—the kinds of structures that are typical of traditionally organized religious groups. These weaknesses likely limit the growth prospects of INC Christianity and ensure that there will always be a market for traditionally organized congregations and denominations. Despite these weaknesses, however, we expect INC Christianity to continue to gain market share relative to traditionally organized religious groups.

Thus, somewhat paradoxically, the macrostructural changes of globalization and the digital revolution give network-oriented forms of religious governance a competitive advantage in terms of growth, yet at the same time limit the possibility that these groups will have a powerful influence on society over the long term.

CHAPTER SEVEN

THE SUCCESS OF INC CHRISTIANITY AND ITS IMPLICATIONS

In the previous chapters, we examined a group of leaders and ministries that we have called Independent Network Charismatic (INC) Christianity and have defined them as a subset neo-Charismatic Christian groups that have the following attributes:

1) *They do not seek to build a "movement"* or to franchise affiliated congregations using a particular name.
2) *They are not primarily focused on building congregations* in the traditional sense, but rather seek to influence the beliefs and practices of followers regardless of congregation or affiliation, including those who are not affiliated with any formal congregation or religious group.
3) *They seek to transform society as a whole* rather than saving individual souls and building congregations.
4) Although they are not formally organized into a "movement" or "denomination," *these high-profile leaders are connected with each other by networks of cooperation.*

Anecdotal information, as well as data from the World Christian Database, suggests that this subset of neo-Charismatic Christianity is one of, if not the, fastest-growing subset of Christianity in the United States and around the world. In the United States, while most other

weak evidence

147

Christian traditions have either declined in absolute numbers or as a percentage of the population, INC Christianity is growing rapidly in both numbers and influence. Although INC Christians still comprise a small percentage of overall Christian believers, it is an important subset to understand because they are one of the few groups that are growing rapidly in the midst of decline for most other religious traditions in the country.

LINKING THE MACROLEVEL AND MESOLEVEL STRUCTURES OF SOCIETY

We posit that the success of INC Christianity is related to changes in the macrostructure of society that have taken place since 1970. Globalization has created an unstable religious marketplace in which multiple worldviews and beliefs are encountered on a daily basis, increasing the state of flux in patterns of religious belief and making many religious groups much more open to reconfiguration.

Digital technology has enabled instant access to information as well as the capacity of individuals to participate in the shaping and creation of knowledge to a much greater degree than was previously possible. These two changes have led, in many sectors of the economy, to the decline of large-scale hierarchical bureaucracies and to the rise of more flexible network-oriented forms of governance among smaller-scale firms and individual actors. These macrolevel social changes have affected the mesolevel religious marketplace in the following ways:

1) Globalization and the resulting cultural pluralism mean there are more religious options than ever, including the possibility of opting out of religious participation altogether.

2) The digital revolution and the unprecedented access to information associated with it have exposed traditional religious organizations to more scrutiny and have opened up new ways for independent religious entrepreneurs to directly access religious "consumers."

148

3) Consumers' greater access to information and a sense of personal empowerment have created a desire for higher levels of lay participation and leadership in practices that are meant to bring about a participant's encounter with the supernatural.

4) Advances in transportation and communications technologies have resulted in greater opportunities for a direct connection between individual leaders and their followers through loose networks that cross state and national boundaries.

These changes in the religious marketplace have given distinct competitive advantages to INC groups in recruiting new followers. These advantages derive from both the beliefs and practices of INC Christianity as well as its governance structures. The competitive advantages that grow out of the unique attributes of INC Christianity can be summarized as follows.

1) THE EXPERIMENTAL NATURE OF INC CHRISTIANITY'S INTERACTION WITH THE SUPERNATURAL

The current competitive and unstable religious marketplace requires groups to offer a compelling product to gain new believers and thereby allow it to "break through the noise" and gain attention in a saturated market. INC Christianity offers consumers an aggressive and intensely experiential form of Christianity. It promises each believer access to direct words of prophecy coming straight from God, to the power to heal diseases and perhaps even raise people from the dead, and to the spiritual ability to drive demonic forces out of individuals, cities, and even nations, liberating them for the rule of God. It also promises participation in a grand project of world transformation through which "heaven on earth" will be established.

Denominational Charismatic and Pentecostal groups make much more modest claims and promises to their constituents. The excessive claims of INC leaders are encouraged by the network structures that shape the flow of authority, power, and money in INC ministries. INC leaders have maximum freedom to make bold claims, hold unorthodox beliefs, and engage in controversial practices because they are not beholden to any organization or authority for their title or position. They market their product directly to the consumer and are connected to other leaders and groups only to the extent that they are able enhance their access to followers. Thus there are no boards, denominations, seminaries, or other institutions that exercise control over or influence the beliefs and practices of INC leaders.

Their status is not dependent on acceptance by other more mainstream religious groups. In fact, a number of recent books by various evangelical writers have criticized the theology and practice of many INC leaders and ministries (see, for example, MacArthur 2013; Geivett and Pivec 2014). These critiques will likely not affect the growing following of INC leaders because their legitimacy and ability to gain followers does not rest on acceptance from the leaders of other traditions. As long as INC leaders can directly market their product to religious consumers in a compelling way, it matters little how much criticism these beliefs and practices get from other movements within Christianity. INC leaders create their own legitimacy through their claims to be apostles and through their ability to produce encounters with the miraculous among their followers.

2) INC CHRISTIANITY IS UNIQUELY WELL SUITED TO MARKET ITS "PRODUCT" OVER THE WEB

INC Christianity has compelling visual content, along with a set of practices that are easily disseminated through web-based media, and offers benefits like "apostolic covering" and "transferable anointing," also known as "impartation," that allow leaders to gain followers (and donors) without the need for brick-and-mortar churches and the attendant liabilities of ownership and institutional affiliation. Other traditions that are more concerned with building congregations, fostering a sense of community and/or formal denominational organizations are less able to leverage the power of the web as effectively because their tasks require more face-to-face communication and local institution building.

3) INC CHRISTIANITY OFFERS A PARTICIPATORY AND EMPOWERING FORM OF RELIGIOUS PRACTICE

Younger generations used to shaping rather than passively consuming ideas and information expect to directly participate in accessing the supernatural and determining the way religion is practiced. INC offers myriad opportunities to participate in public expressions of faith. Because the primary forms of expression (prayer, prophecy, healing, spiritual warfare) are not confined to a congregation or church building, there are unlimited opportunities for lay members to go out and "do stuff," as we heard numerous times from participants.

4) THE NETWORK FORM OF GOVERNANCE ALLOWS INC LEADERS TO ACCESS RESOURCES FROM A WIDER POOL OF DONORS AND SPEND RESOURCES PRIMARILY ON ACTIVITIES THAT EXPAND RATHER THAN MERELY MAINTAIN THEIR MARKET SHARE

Multilevel vertical networks give high-profile individual leaders access to donations from potentially thousands of congregations and millions of followers, whereas pastors of traditional congregations must rely primarily on their own congregation for donations. In addition, members of a traditional congregation expect services, programs from which they personally benefit and a sense of belonging in return for their financial support and participation. INC followers and donors expect only that the spiritual power flowing from the anointed leader will trickle down to them in some way, and that they will acquire access to power through various learned techniques.

The results of these activities are difficult to quantify, and true believers trust in the power of their leaders and techniques, even in the face of questionable evidence. Thus INC leaders can spend their resources on promotional materials that further expand their following and resources—conferences, media productions, live-streamed broadcasts, and books—rather than on creating and maintaining programs and services for a local congregation. Networks of leaders can join together for short-term projects to enhance the audience for these promotional materials and events, allowing them to expand the reach of their following. If a relationship goes sour between leaders, or if a leader is caught up in a scandal, the network can simply reconfigure itself without the problematic leader and continue promoting collaboration among the remaining leaders as well as cultivating new leadership.

NETWORKS IN THE RELIGIOUS ECONOMY

All of these sources of competitive advantage are related to the governance structure of INC Christianity as a network of leaders, as opposed to traditionally organized congregations and denominations. All of the high-profile leaders we examined have "ministries" that are nonprofit organizations as well as large congregations that are typically listed under the ministry name. For example, Che Ahn's HROCK church is a part of his nonprofit organization Harvest International Ministries (HIM). The same is the case with Bill Johnson's Bethel and Mike Bickle's International House of Prayer. As IRS tax-exempt nonprofit organizations, each of these leaders must have a board of trustees. In each of these organizations, however, it was clear that the founder and "apostle" has the ultimate say in the decisions of the organization. The board and leadership teams looked to the founder to set the agenda.

These ministries are all headed by highly respected charismatic leaders who are in regular contact with other leaders running similar INC organizations. Some have come to formal agreements to work together, such as the members of the "Revival Alliance." More common are informal relationships in which the leaders communicate regularly and cooperate on short-term projects. Some sit on each other's boards of trustees. Thus these organizations are all legally independent of any overarching authority and led strongly by a single individual. Some leaders form "vertical" networks with a clear hierarchy, and others form "horizontal" networks of cooperation in which no leader has authority over the others. Leaders can move in and out of relationship with other leaders with no legal ramifications. If a leader falls out of favor with other leaders, such as in the case of Todd Bentley and the Revival Alliance, the leader can quickly align with other leaders in another network to regain his or her footing.

Jones et al. (1997) define network governance as "a select, persistent, and structured set of autonomous firms (as well as nonprofit agencies) engaged in creating products or services based on implicit and open-ended contracts to adapt to environmental contingencies and to coordinate and safeguard exchanges. These contracts are socially—not legally—binding." By "select," they mean that the network does not comprise an entire sector or industry, but rather a subset of firms that work together for short-term projects. By "persistent" they mean that these alliances are not simply one-time instances of cooperation, but operate fairly consistently over long periods of time. Borrowing from Powell (1990), they posit that network governance represents a "distinct form of coordinating economic activity" (Powell 1990; 301), which contrasts (and competes) with markets and hierarchies.

A substantial body of literature has emerged in the last thirty years to describe the emergence of network governance in global capitalism. Authors have used slightly different terms—for example, "network organization" (Miles and Snow 1986), "network forms of organization" (Powell 1990), "interfirm networks" and "organization networks" (Uzzi 1996; 1997), "flexible specialization" (Piore and Sabel 1984), and "quasi-firms" (Eccles, 1981)—to describe this transition away from reliance on intrafirm bureaucracies or formal contractual agreements between firms in the production of goods and services (Gerlach 1992; Nohria 1992).

Jones et al. (1997) identify four conditions in which network governance tends to emerge, thrive, and outperform other forms of leadership:

1) *Demand uncertainty*: Firms cooperate to reduce fixed costs and increase flexibility when the demand for products changes rapidly.

2) *The need for customized products involving high human-asset specificity*: The creation of customized products to meet shifting

consumer demands requires the acquisition of human assets—people who are uniquely experienced in creating customized products—as opposed to people trained in standardized production methods. The unique and specific skills needed for a highly customized product are often more easily assembled through a network than within a bureaucracy.

3) *The need to complete complex tasks under time pressure*: Producing a product quickly to meet changing market demands requires the cooperation of multiple skilled participants, who can act more easily and quickly in a network than in a bureaucracy.

4) *The need for frequent exchanges between firms*: When firms need to exchange goods and services frequently over time, relationships of trust are needed to prevent firms from committing acts of narrow self-interest at the expense of their exchange partner.

The religious economy in the United States during this time of flux is arguably experiencing all four of these conditions. First, demand for religious "services" is unstable, particularly among young adults. In this environment, it becomes more important to offer more customized and compelling religious "products" to grow the number of followers in a declining and competitive market. This requires "human-asset specificity" in the form of uniquely gifted and talented leaders who have the ability to access and promote the supernatural in unconventional ways.

Standardized sermons coming from standardized methods of interpreting scripture, learned at denominational seminaries, overlain with routinized forms of worship coming from traditionally organized congregations, form a recipe for decline in the current unstable religious market. This puts a higher premium on innovative, dynamic leaders with Weberian charisma.

Networks of dynamic leaders and their associates are also much better equipped to accomplish complex tasks under time pressure than are traditional congregations or denominations. Creating a sports-arena-scale prayer rally like Rick Perry's "Response" or

Lou Engle's "Azusa Now," for example, would be difficult for a denomination like the Southern Baptist Convention (SBC) to pull off, even if they would largely support the idea and agenda motivating these rallies. Specifically, there would be too many rules and committees slowing down the process to allow the SBC to get the program approved and pulled together on short notice. Moreover, a denominational body would probably not be able, using its own resources, to assemble enough high-profile speakers and politicians to attract a crowd that would fill a football stadium. Securing the funding for such an event would also be a problem for a traditional denomination. By contrast, the INC organizers drew on a network of high-profile and well-connected INC leaders, as well as leaders from other traditions and organizations, who could quickly assemble a collaboration focused on a single project, then disassemble that ad hoc network to free up the potential to undertake subsequent projects.

Trust relationships are also important in establishing a growing religious group. In putting together a high-profile conference, for example, that entails bringing in popular INC leaders from around the world, one would need to trust that the speakers would not say anything that would go against the spirit and values of the conference—and trust that the leaders would be cooperative rather than self-interested at the expense of others. Networks allow for long-term trust relationships to be built over time among high-profile leaders through frequent exchanges of services and resources.

One way to view the rise of INC Christianity therefore is to see the network governance structure as compatible with the externalities of the current religious marketplace, which is characterized by unstable and dwindling demand for religious services, particularly among young people. Another more provocative way to think about it is to see it as part of a larger-scale transformation toward a "network society."

Castells (2000) and others (Barney 2004; Van Dijk 2006) have taken the arguments for the advantages of network governance under certain circumstances a step further. They assert that the world has become a network society as a result of advances in digital communications technologies.

Castells (2004) defines a network society as "a society whose social structure is made of networks powered by microelectronics-based information and communication technologies." These authors do not argue that networks are somehow new to twenty-first-century societies. Indeed, the importance of social networks in commerce, politics, and culture has been long established. They do argue, however, that until the "information revolution" of the late twentieth century, large vertically integrated bureaucracies were superior in mobilizing people, resources, and power for most of human history.

Still, networks have always been an effective form of organizing collective efforts. Their main advantages are their flexibility and adaptability. Their main limitation, however, has been their limited capacity to mobilize large numbers of people and resources for large-scale complex tasks (Castells & Cardoso 2005). In the transition to modernity, power shifted to those societies and groups that could rationally organize large-scale tasks such as military conquest, economic production, and political mobilization through routinized formal organizations. This is what impressed Weber about modernity. He saw little hope for escape from the "iron cage" of bureaucracy because large-scale formalized organizations—whether militaries, nation–states, corporations, or religious denominations—would eventually eliminate all of their smaller-scale, less-organized competitors through their superior ability to organize and mobilize resources and people in pursuit of their purposes.

In the last two decades, however, new theories have emerged that argue that the advent of digital communications technologies has created new ways of organizing large numbers of people around a common goal. The ability of people and groups to communicate easily and quickly over large distances has increased the capacity of networks to mobilize people and resources while still retaining their inherent flexibility and adaptability (Castells and Cardoso 2005). Thus the coordination of a large, decentralized network of actors outside of a formal organization to complete a task is now possible.

Castells (2004) claims that because of advances in digital communications technologies, networks now have the following advantages over large bureaucracies:

1) Flexibility: Networks can reconfigure themselves according to changing environments, keeping their goals while changing their components. They automatically flow past blockages in communication channels to find new connections.
2) Scalability: They can expand or shrink in size with little disruption.
3) Survivability: Because they have no central organizational authority and can operate in a wide range of configurations, networks can resist attacks on their nodes and "codes" (knowledge and practices) because the codes of the network are contained in multiple nodes that can reproduce the instructions and find new ways to perform. So only the physical ability to destroy the connecting points can eliminate the network.

We have seen that INC groups have these advantages over traditionally organized religious groups. They can configure and reconfigure for short-term or long-term projects. When an "outpouring of the spirit" occurs such as the Toronto Blessing or the Lakeland Florida revival, the network can marshal its considerable resources—including TV and live-stream coverage, financial support, logistics and high-profile speakers—to organize programming around that venue or location. When the "outpouring" subsides, another event, such as the outpouring in Kansas City, can take its place. INC networks are "scalable"— they can increase or decrease in size depending on the task at hand. When organizing a large, complex event such as "Azusa Now," the network can expand and involve large numbers of high-profile leaders. For smaller tasks or events, such as a prophecy conference at a local church, the organizing group can be much smaller and may not require high-profile speakers, along with the logistical apparatus that their participation entails.

The third characteristic in Castells's list of advantages, "survivability," is particularly important for religious groups. Often religious groups are only as stable as their primary leader. If the head pastor of a church leaves, dies, or succumbs to scandal or impropriety, the congregation is often damaged and in danger of collapse. If the congregation is part of a larger formal denomination, that denomination may also pay a price, depending on how the denominational leadership handles the scandal or leadership transition. INC networks, however, can survive scandals with less damage because each leader operates independently of the other leaders. Two scandals serve as examples.

High-profile INC leaders Todd Bentley and Ted Haggard were both involved in scandals related to sexual impropriety. Both disappeared from the conference and revival circuit and were essentially dismissed from their ministries. This caused little damage to the networks in which they were involved, however, because their followers simply aligned with another apostle and joined a different INC group.

Haggard's New Life Church in Colorado Springs, under new leadership, is still one of the largest churches in the United States. Bentley's highly publicized revivals have been eclipsed by revivals breaking out elsewhere. Even though the INC network structure seems to increase the possibility for corruption and scandal, it also reduces scandal-related damage to the resources of the network as a whole. When one node of the network is eliminated because of scandal, other nodes quickly fill the gap with little effect on the network as a whole.

This is not to say, however, that the organization and expansion of religious groups through networks of independent actors is a new phenomenon. Kim and Pfaff (2012) demonstrate convincingly that the Protestant Reformation itself was formed by a network of university students who were able to bridge "structural holes" (Burt 1992) between reformist university professors and urban religious communities. Indeed, the typical pattern of the birth of religious movements throughout history is that they begin as a network of unorthodox leaders who diffuse ideas across "structural holes" to gain a larger following. Stark's (1996) work on the rise of Christianity demonstrates that the movement started as a network of independent leaders who spread novel ideas and organized collective action, but then eventually established formal institutions. Fundamentalism also emerged as a network of independent evangelists, Bible institutes, and Bible conferences in the early twentieth century, as the movement's followers sought to hold on to traditional theological ideas in the face of challenges from modernity (Marsden 2006).

As we have shown in Chapter 2, the neo-Charismatic movement itself began as a network of leaders, such as those in the Jesus Movement, which eventually organized congregations and denominational associations like Calvary Chapel and the Vineyard (Miller 1997). Although we acknowledge the network-based origins of all new religious movements, we see INC Christianity as different because its leaders are actively seeking to preserve the network structure as an ongoing governance strategy, openly rejecting the idea of organizing into an institution, or set of institutions, with more formal governance structures.

Other religious movements in history were not necessarily ideologically opposed to formal governance structures, as is the case with INC leaders. Nor were they able to mobilize large numbers of people on a global scale through network structures to the extent that INC groups do because of advances in digital communications technology. Whether these leaders and groups will eventually form into denomination-like structures is an open question. Some probably will. But others seem likely to continue to grow and gain followers without a formal governance structure. Indeed, those that are able to resist developing such a structure will probably continue to grow faster than those that become more routinized.

THE FUTURE OF PROTESTANTISM?

INC Christianity is arguably the fastest-growing segment of Christianity in the United States, and possibly in the world. Because of INC Christianity's competitive advantages in a globalized, wired, and networked society, it appears that it will continue to grow faster than other more traditionally organized religious groups and thus continue to gain market share in comparison with other traditions. What is less clear is whether this form of Christianity, or at least some aspects of it, will eventually become the dominant form of Protestantism in the future.

INC Christianity currently occupies a fast-growing but still fairly small niche in American and global Christianity. Although this niche will certainly continue to expand, the weaknesses we identified in Chapter 6 may ultimately limit its growth potential. Some followers of INC leaders will likely drop out as they become disillusioned with the INC product, if and when it fails to deliver on some of its promises of supernatural healing, the liberation of geographic areas from demonic influence, and the transmission of messages from God. Others will likely return to traditionally organized congregations as they grow older and feel the need for more basic and less spectacular religious goods such as access to stable, long-term community relationships and programming for families and kids. Still others will likely begin to question the absolute authority and financing strategies of high-profile INC apostles.

Although it is impossible to predict how dominant in the religious marketplace INC Christianity will become in the future, it seems likely that other religious groups will adopt at least some of the innovative methods, governance structures, and practices of INC networks. The theory of institutional isomorphism states that, in unstable environments, organizations will copy the practices and structures of groups that are most successful (DiMaggio and Powell 1983). If other religious groups are to avoid decline in this highly competitive and unstable religious marketplace, they must address the following issues that INC leaders have successfully negotiated:

1) *Offer a compelling experience of the supernatural*

If anything is clear from our interviews with young participants in INC Christianity, it is that its followers are not satisfied with religion that only engages their minds with theologies and concepts about God. A congregation structured around the passive learning of information about God is almost inevitably doomed to fail in an information-saturated, experience-hungry social context. Experiences of authentic personal interaction with the supernatural and the divine seem to "break through" the noise and distraction for over-stimulated young people. Practices that engage the body, the senses, the emotions and the spirit are key attractions to INC Christianity that could be engaged and replicated in any number of ways.

What is clear is that religious practices centered on a long sermon from a highly educated expert on theological matters seems likely to continue to lose market share. This does not mean that Bible teaching or theology per se is doomed to market failure. It simply means that they do not provide a compelling enough experience, standing alone, to generate growth in the current religious marketplace. Traditionally organized congregations therefore need to find ways to combine compelling experiences that engage the body, emotions, and spirit with those that engage the mind.

2) *Create opportunities for public expression of beliefs and practices*

One of the primary attractions of INC Christianity is that its leaders have developed practices that are meant for expression in the public sphere, rather than in the context of a church service. Healing the sick and offering words of prophecy in public places, as well as prayer rallies and marches that confront "territorial spirits," fulfill a desire for a public faith that is not relegated to the private sphere of home, family, and church. INC leaders have effectively conveyed the message that their followers are involved in a grand project of social transformation—of bringing "heaven to earth" in ways that many traditional congregations have failed to do.

Evangelical Christianity, in particular, typically has a more privatized agenda—saving individual souls for heaven and building up the institutional church are its key tasks. A public expression of faith could take a number of forms other than the supernatural public expression of INC groups. Examples might include more traditional public expressions of faith such as social service, political action, and commitment to social reform. Traditionally organized groups whose primary focus is on saving souls, but that do not offer opportunities for followers to be part of a larger project that has public implications, seem likely to lose followers among a generation that yearns to participate in a larger project with public, world-changing implications.

3) *Allow followers to lead*

Because INC Christianity promotes a set of practices that any "spirit-filled" person can perform, and because these practices are performed in public—not just in church—there are unlimited opportunities for followers to participate in and even lead their own ministries. Because INC leaders are not formally affiliated with their followers through a church or denominational bureaucracy, they can encourage lay leaders to experiment with practices in public without worrying about the potential for criticism. They are encouraged to "go out and do stuff." INC practices have the advantage of not needing much organizational support—anyone can show up at a hospital or park and pray for people to be healed.

Traditionally organized groups that do not provide opportunities for new young believers to participate in and lead activities and ministries are likely to lose followers. In a highly regulated church service, there are only so many slots for leadership—whether it be leading worship, preaching, or reading scripture. The rest of the congregation is resigned to passively consume what others provide. In a ministry designed to serve the public, however, there are unlimited opportunities for young leaders to emerge. In a social context in which "experiential consuming" (Florida 2002) leads to the expectation that consumers will interact with and personally shape the information and products they consume, they are not likely to be satisfied with a religious faith where there are few opportunities to participate in shaping the direction of religious practice.

4) *Seek new financial models*

INC Christianity has a built-in financial advantage over traditionally organized religious groups. Traditionally organized groups rely heavily on Sunday service plate donations to fund their operations. This financing model requires a stable congregation that is willing to contribute substantially to the ministry. As a result, much of the activity of the leadership must focus on recruiting and retaining Sunday morning attendees. This congregation-centric model limits the amount of revenue that can be raised for the activities outside of the congregation and keeps the focus on intracongregational programming rather than on public activities that can draw new followers (Smith, Emerson, and Snell 2008). The declining number of members who contribute financially to congregations and the shrinking percentage of income that followers give to charitable causes make financing congregation-based ministries difficult.

INC groups, in contrast, raise the bulk of their funds from sources outside of their congregations—the sale of media products, conference tickets, curriculum materials, and live-stream web broadcasts fuels the budgets of INC groups. In addition, interns and ministry school students pay to participate in many INC programs. Some observers might see this transformation of religious groups into "pay-for-service" programs as ethically problematic. Still, because INC groups are not primarily concerned with building congregations, they can raise money from a wider array of sources and spend that revenue to expand their following rather than to maintain programs internal to a congregation. These techniques cannot be easily replicated in a congregation-based religious group because, by definition, if building congregations is the focus, it would be difficult to raise and spend money on activities outside of the congregation. Thus, apart from megachurches with celebrity pastors, congregation-based religious groups will likely remain at a financial disadvantage compared with groups in which leaders appeal directly to followers outside of a congregation.

Furthermore, because INC groups are not primarily concerned with building congregations, they can keep overhead costs associated with staffing a congregation to a minimum and spend more resources on activities that promise to enlarge their following. This points toward the possibility that if more of the activities of traditional groups focused on public practices that lay people could lead—prayer, evangelism, or serving their communities, for example—less resources would need to be spent on staffing programs to serve congregational members themselves.

Traditionally organized congregations and denominations could address these issues without giving unlimited authority to dynamic individual leaders and without abandoning the local congregation as the center of religious life. This would allow congregations to gain market share without experiencing some of the liabilities of INC Christianity's governance structures, beliefs, and practices.

The essential tension we have identified in our study is rooted in the question of who holds the ultimate power to make decisions in a religious group—an individual or the group itself. There are dangerous pitfalls on both sides of question. Giving too much power to dynamic individual religious entrepreneurs can lead to beliefs and practices that drift too far outside of the realm of believability, ultimately limiting their long-term appeal. It also can lead to the abuse of power and wealth. A network of individuals is also limited in its ability to effect long-term social change. On the other hand, giving too much power to formal bureaucracies often leads to an overly cautious and constricted religion that loses its ability to experiment with the supernatural and the divine in ways that can inspire new followers.

One of the benefits of a pluralistic religious marketplace is that it allows for experimentation and innovation in the way a given group structures its religious beliefs and practices. In a competitive religious marketplace it is more likely that, over time, beliefs and practices that benefit followers in some way will continue to grow and spread, whereas those that harm followers, or that simply do not deliver what they have promised, will fade over time.

This is not to say that the beliefs and practices that gain market share over time are necessarily "true" or those that fail to inspire new followers in a particular social context are "false." It also could be the case that practices that gain market share are harmful to religious consumers and society as a whole. It seems true, however, that forms of religious expression that have perceived benefits to followers them-selves will grow in popularity over time. Perhaps new religious forms will emerge in the future that retain the perceived benefits of INC Christianity (direct engagement with the supernatural, new methods of using technology to spread beliefs and practices, allowing direct

[handwritten annotations: ridiculous to list two as a "benefit" w/o assuming how big/small is demand for supernatural]

participation and leadership among lay people) while jettisoning those that produce outcomes that are perceived to be negative or harmful.

The cost of unregulated religious markets is that people can be exploited, deceived and sometimes abused at the hands of powerful religious leaders. This may be a potential cost that is worth the gains that come from experimentation and innovation. The net result seems to be that at least some of the population of believers experiences the divine and the supernatural in ways that would not be possible in a highly regulated marketplace. The upside is that people are able to experience the divine in new ways that—for most, we hope—outweigh any collateral damage.

CONCLUSION

In this book we have made the case that the macrosocial structural transformations that have taken place since the 1970s have led to mesolevel changes in the religious marketplace in the United States. These changes have led to the rise of networks of independent religious entrepreneurs that we have called INC Christianity, which are gaining market share relative to traditionally organized congregations and denominations in an increasingly unstable religious economy. We predict that religious groups that are organized around networks will continue to gain market share in the near future, while traditionally organized denominations and congregations will continue to lose market share. If that is the case, what does it mean for the future of religion?

We propose four hypotheses that may grow from other religious groups' imitating the network structure of INC Christianity and some of its associated practices. First, *religious belief and practice will become increasingly experimental*. Without institutions such as denominations, seminaries, and church boards that have the authority and legitimacy to regulate their beliefs and practices, individual charismatic leaders will continue to develop unorthodox ways of connecting to the divine that will attract new followers. In a competitive and saturated market, religious beliefs and practices that are novel and that promise more "extreme" encounters with the supernatural will become more commonplace, as information-saturated seekers look for increasingly dramatic experiences. Second, *authority and power in religious groups will become more highly concentrated in the hands of individuals rather than institutions.* Dynamic charismatic leaders who can appeal directly to the "consumer" without needing the backing of formally organized religious institutions will have much more autonomy and influence in the religious marketplace, as they are the ultimate authority in their ministries.

Third, *religion will become more oriented toward practice rather than theology.* Religious consumers increasingly expect to practice their faith in public settings in their own customized ways. Religion that is focused on learning doctrine and theology from highly trained experts will continue to become less compelling to an increasingly information-saturated population. Religion, as a result, will be defined increasingly as something a person does rather than something a person knows or believes. Finally, *religious beliefs and practices will become more interactive and customized by the individual consumer than by the governing authorities of a religious tradition of which they are a part.* Beliefs and practices will increasingly look like "experiential consumption" (Florida 2002), in which participants are cocreators of the religious practices in which they engage. This will lead to the multiplication of many public expressions of faith as individuals and groups customize their practice by drawing from multiple resources and create practices that reflect their own personal interests and passions.

We also predict that, as networked forms of organization among religious groups continue to grow, there will be a steadily increasing backlash among traditionalists and therefore perhaps a modest return migration of believers to established denominations, along with a renewed emphasis on doctrine, theological beliefs, and the congregation as the center of religious life. There will always be a market for traditionally organized religion. That said, we believe that INC Christianity and its networked form of organization will continue to gain market share compared with traditionally organized groups, exerting an increasingly strong influence on the way that Christianity as well as other religious traditions are experienced and practiced. We leave it to theologians and religious practitioners to debate whether or not these on balance are healthy developments. We simply assert that network-based religion will continue to grow and profoundly influence the way religion is practiced in the future.

REFERENCES

Assemblies of God. 1949. "Resolution 7: The New Order of the Latter Rain." *Minutes of the General Council of the Assemblies of God.* Retrieved April 6, 2015. (http://Ifphc.org/DigitalPublications/USA/).

Assemblies of God. 2000. "Endtime Revival-Spirit-Led and Spirit-Controlled: A Response Paper to Resolution 16." Retrieved April 6, 2015. (http://ag.org/top/Beliefs/Position_Papers/pp_downloads/pp_endtime_revival.pdf).

Barney, D. 2004. *The Network Society.* Oxford, UK: Polity.

Bellah, R. N., R. Madsen, W. M. Sullivan, A. Swidler, and S. M. Tipton. 1985. *Habits of the Heart: Individualism and Commitment in American Life.* Berkeley and Los Angeles: University of California Press.

Berger, Peter. 1967. *The Sacred Canopy: Elements of a Sociological Theory of Religion.* Garden City, NY: Doubleday.

Bernstein, Elizabeth. 2007. "The Sexual Politics of the 'New Abolitionism.'" *Differences: A Journal of Feminist Cultural Studies* 18(3):18–151.

Burnett, Ron. 2005. *How Images Think.* Cambridge, MA: MIT Press.

Burt, Ronald S. 1992. *Structural Holes.* Cambridge, MA: Harvard University Press.

Carpenter, Joel A. 2003. "Compassionate Evangelicalism." *Christianity Today* 47(12): 40–42.

Castells, Manuel. 2004. *The Network Society: A Cross Cultural Perspective.* Cheltenham, UK: Elgar.

Castells, Manuel. 2000. *The Rise of the Network Society: The Information Age: Economy Society and Culture Volume 1.* 2nd Ed. West Sussex, UK: Wiley.

Castells, Manuel and Gustavo Cardoso. 2005. *The Network Society: From Knowledge to Policy*. Washington, DC: Johns Hopkins Center for Transatlantic Relations.

Chu, Jeff. 2010. "How Willow Creek is Leading Evangelicals by Learning from the Business World." *Fast Company* 151 (January 2010). Retrieved April 6, 2015. (http://www.fastcompany.com/magazine/151/december-2010-january-2010).

DiMaggio, P. J. and W. W. Powell. 1983. "The Iron Cage Revisited: Institutional Isomorphism and Cellective Rationality in Organizational Fields." *American Sociological Review* 48(2):147–160.

DiSabatino, David. 1999. *The Jesus People Movement*. Westport, CT: Greenwood.

Eccles, R. G. 1981. "The Quasifirm in the Construction Industry." *Journal of Economic Behavior and Organization* 2: 335–357.

Emerson, Michael O. and Christian Smith. 2000. *Divided by Faith: Evangelical Religion and the Problem of Race in America*. New York: Oxford University Press.

Finke, Roger and Rodney Stark. 1992. *The Churching of America 1776–1990: Winners and Losers in Our Religious Economy*. New Brunswick, NJ: Rutgers University Press.

Florida, Richard. 2002. *The Rise of the Creative Class*. New York: Basic Books.

Flory, Richard and Kimon Sargeant. 2013. "Pentecostalism in Global Perspective." Pp. 297–317 in *Spirit and Power: The Growth and Global Impact of Pentecostalism*, edited by Flory and Seargeant. New York: Oxford University Press.

Flory, Richard and Donald E. Miller. 2008. *Finding Faith: The Spiritual Quest of the Post-Boomer Generation*. New Brunswick, NJ: Rutgers University Press.

Gaines, Adrienne S. 2009. "Todd Bentley Remarries, Begins Restoration Process." *Charisma Magazine*. March 10, 2009. Retrieved April 1, 2015. (http://www.charismamag.com/site-archives/570-news/featured-news/3974-todd-bentley-remarries-begins-restoration-process).

Geivett, R. Douglas and Holly Pivec. 2014. *A New Apostolic Reformation? A Biblical Response to a Worldwide Movement*. Wooster, OH: Weaver.

Gereffi, G. 1996. "Global Commodity Chains: New Forms of Coordination and Control among Nations and Firms in International Industries: *Competition and Change* 1: 427–439.

Gerlach, M. L. 1992. "The Japanese Corporate Network: A Blockmodel Analysis." *Administrative Science Quarterly* 37: 105–139.

Gerson, Michael. 2006. "A New Social Gospel." *Newsweek* 148(20): 40–43.

Green, J. C., J. L. Guth, C. E. Smidt, and L. A. Kellstedt. 1997. *Religion and Culture Wars*. Lanham, MD: Rowman and Littlefield.

Hamilton, M. S. 2000. "Willow Creek's Place in History." *Christianity Today* 44(13): 62–69.

Hansen, Mark B. N. 2004. *New Philosophy for New Media*. Cambridge, MA: MIT Press.

Heimans, J. and H. Timms. 2014. "Understanding 'New Power.'" *Harvard Business Review*, December. Retrieved March 2, 2016. (https://hbr.org/2014/12/understanding-Trumpets?new-power).

Johnson, Miles E. 2016. "Ted Cruz Trumpets Endorsement From a Man Who Thinks God Sent Hitler to Hunt the Jews." *Mother Jones* January 26, 2016. Retrieved March 1, 2016. (http://www.motherjones.com/mojo/2016/01/).

Jones, C., W. S. Hesterly, and S. P. Borgatti. 1997. "A General Theory of Network Governance: Exchange Conditions and Social Mechanisms." *Academy of Management Review* 22(4): 911–945.

Kay, William. 2007. *Apostolic Networks in Britain*. Milton Keynes, UK: Paternoster.

Keckler, C. and M. J. Rozell. 2015. "The Libertarian Right and the Religious Right." *Perspectives on Political Science* 44(2): 92–99.

Kim, Hyojoung and Steven Pfaff. 2012. "Structure and Dynamics of Religious Insurgency: Students and the Spread of the Reformation." *American Sociological Review* 77(2): 188–215.

Kraft, Charles. 2005. *SWM/SIS at Forty: A Participant/Observers View of Our History*. Pasadena, CA: William Carey Library Press.

Lord, Andy. 2012. *Network Church: A Pentecostal Ecclesiology Shaped by Mission*. Boston: Brill.

Marsden, George. 2006. *Fundamentalism and American Culture*. 2nd Ed. New York: Oxford University Press.

MacArthur, John. 2013. *Strange Fire: The Danger of Offending the Holy Spirit with Counterfeit Worship*. Nashville, TN: Nelson.

McMullen, Cary. 2008. "Florida Outpouring: Internet Draws Thousands to Lakeland Revival. *The Ledger* May 18. Retrieved April 10, 2015. (http://www.theledger.com/article/2008518/NEWS/805180341/1004).

Miles, R. E.and C. C. Snow.1986. "Organizations: New Concepts for New Forms." *California Management Review* 28(3): 62–73.

Miller, Donald. 1997. *Reinventing American Protestantism: Christianity in the New Millennium*. Berkeley: University of California Press

Miller, Donald and Tetsunao Yamamori. 2007. *Global Pentecostalism: The New Face of Christian Social Engagement*. Berkeley: University of California Press.

Nohria, N. 1992. "Is Network Perspective a Useful Way of Studying Organizations?" Pp. 1–22 in *Networks and Organizations: Structure, Form, and Action*, edited by N. Nohria and R. G. Eccles. Boston: Harvard Business School Press.

Ong, Czarina. 2015. "Donald Trump Gets Prophetic Prayer From Christian Teacher Who Likens Him to Cyrus, God's Anointed Leader." *Christianity Today* November 6, 2015. Retrieved March 1, 2016 (http://www.christianitytoday.com).

Pew Research Center. 2012. "Nones on the Rise." Religion and Public Life web page. Retrieved March 20, 2015. (http://www.pewforum.org).

Piore, M. J. and C. F. Sabel.1984. *The Second Industrial Divide*. New York: Basic Books.

Poloma, Margaret. 1989. *The Assemblies of God at the Crossroads*. Knoxville: University of Tennessee Press.

Poloma, Margaret. 2003. *Main Street Mystics: Toronto Blessing and Reviving Pentecostalism*. Walnut Creek, CA: Alta Mira.

Powell, W. 1990. "Neither Market nor Hierarchy: Network Forms of Organization." *Research in Organizational Behavior* 12: 295–336.

Price, Paula A. 1994. *God's Apostle Revived*. Plainfield, NJ: Everlasting Life Publications.

Ryan, Marie-Laure. 2003. *Narrative as Virtual Reality: Immersion and Interactivitiy in Literature and Electronic Media*. Baltimore, MD: Johns Hopkins University Press.

Sargeant, Kimon H. 2000. *Seeker Churches: Promoting Traditional Religion in a Nontraditional Way*. New Brunswick, NJ: Rutgers University Press.

Schnabel, L. P. 2013. "When Fringe Goes Mainstream: A Sociohistorical Content Analysis of the Christian Coalition's Contract With The American Family and the Republican Party Platform." *Politics, Religion, and Ideology* 14(1): 94–113.

Sherket, D. E. and C. G. Ellison. 1999. "Recent Developments and Current Controversies in the Sociology of Religion." *Annual Review of Sociology* 25: 363–394.

Smith, Christian with Michael Emerson, Sally Gallagher, Paul Kennedy, and David Sikkink. 1998. *American Evangelicalism: Embattled and Thriving*. Chicago: University of Chicago Press.

Smith, Christian, Michael O. Emerson, and Patricia Snell. 2008. *Passing the Plate: Why American Christians Don't Give Away More Money*. New York: Oxford University Press.

Stafford, Tim. 2012. "Miracles in Mozambique." *Christianity Today* 56(5): 18–26.

Stark, Rodney. 1996. *The Rise of Christianity*. Princeton, NJ: Princeton University Press.

Stark, R. and W. S. Bainbridge. 1987. *A Theory of Religion*. Toronto: Lang.

Stetzer, Ed. 2014. "A Catalyst That Fostered a Movement: Thoughts on Bob Buford and Leadership Network." *Christianity Today*. Online Version Retrieved April 6, 2015 (http://www.christianitytoday.com/edstatzer/2014/april/catalyst-that-fostered-movement.html).

Tapscott, Don. 1998. *Growing Up Digital: The Rise of the Net Generation*. New York: McGraw-Hill.

U.S. Congregational Life Survey. 2008. Retrieved April 8, 2015. (http://www.presbyterian.typepad.com/beyondordinary/2011/05/where-deos-the-money-come-from-financing-the-local-church-.html).

Uzzi, B. 1996. "Embeddedness in the Making of Financial Capital: How Social Relations and Networks Benefit Firms Seeking Financing." *American Sociological Review* 64: 481–505.

Uzzi, B. 1997. "Social Structure and Competition in Interfirm Networks: The Paradox of Embededness." *Administrative Science Quarterly* 42: 35–67.

Van Dijk, Jan A. G. M. 2006. *The Network Society: Social Aspects of New Media*. 2nd Ed. London: Sage.

Wagner, C. Peter. 2010. *Wrestling With Alligators, Prophets, and Theologians: Lessons From a Lifetime in the Church*. Ventura, CA: Regal.

Wagner, C. Peter. 2006. *Apostles Today: Biblical Government for Biblical Power.* Ventura, CA: Regal.

Weber, Max. 1978. *Economy and Society: An Outline of Interpretive Sociology.* Edited by Guenther Roth and Claus Wittich. Berkeley, CA: University of California Press.

Wilkinson, Michael and Peter Althouse. 2014. *Catch the Fire: Soaking Prayer and Charismatic Renewal.* DeKalb, IL: Northern Illinois University Press.

INDEX

Tables, figures, and boxes are indicated by an italic t, f, and b following the page/
paragraph number.

relationship and work with Wagner, 20, 21, 27–28, 29; and religious economy paradigm, 41–42; teaches Fuller classes, 21–22; writings of, 61. *See also* Anaheim Vineyard

WLI. *See* Wagner Leadership Institute (WLI)

workplace apostles, 138

World Christian Database (WCD), 3–4*t*, 4–5, 8–9, 147

Yamamori, Tetsunao, 45

Yoido Full Gospel Church, 10

Yorba Linda Friends Church, 19–20, 27

young adults: attraction to social transformation, 91–101; attractiveness of INC Christianity among, 80–81, 84, 85–90, 102, 103–4, 160–61; impact of social changes on, 15–16; new power and technology, 102–3; religious affiliation of, 2–3. *See also* internship programs

Youth With a Mission (YWAM), 6, 79; as alternative to traditional congregations, 81; challenges for members with families, 133; Discipleship Training Schools, 112, 118; finance and marketing innovations in, 112; internship programs, 118–19; participatory and empowering form of practice, 89–90; within Spiritual Warfare Network, 29

Printed in the USA/Agawam, MA
August 10, 2018

680540.014